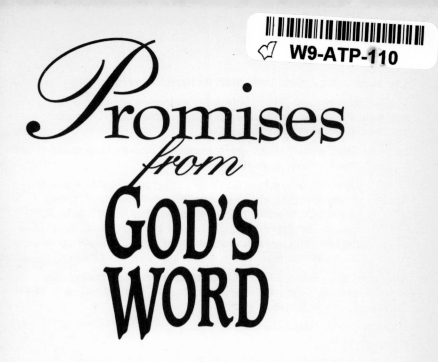

Promises *from* GOD'S WORD

This Billy Graham Evangelistic Association special edition is published with permission from World Publishing, Inc.

WORLD PUBLISHING

Grand Rapids, Michigan 49418 U.S.A.

W9-ATP-110

Developed and produced by the Livingstone Corporation. Project staff include: James C. Galvin, Christopher D. Hudson, Diane Krusemark, Mary Ann Lackland, and Brenda J. Todd.

Cover design by JMK Associates

ISBN 0-913367-66-4

Library of Congress Catalog Card Number 96-60098

Published by: World Publishing, Inc.
                Grand Rapids, Michigan 49418 U.S.A.
                All rights reserved.

Printed in the United States of America

❧ TABLE OF CONTENTS ❧

❧ INTRODUCTION ❧

Life can be painful. Throughout every year, friends fail us, family members disappoint us, and coworkers hurt us. Other frustrations, accidents, and sicknesses disrupt the flow of our lives. During these difficult times, we need reminders that God cherishes, loves, protects, and cares for his children.

Promises from GOD'S WORD was compiled to help you during these times. You'll find topics that relate to the experiences and emotions that you may face each day. Each topic contains Scripture readings that relate to you and your situation.

Use this book of Bible promises for:

1) *Personal comfort*: When you need to feel God's warm care.

2) *Personal devotions*: When you want to apply God's word to your life.

3) *Personal or group study*: When you want to learn more about God, or teach a Bible study or Sunday school lesson.

All the readings come from the easy-to-read Bible translation, *GOD'S WORD*™. In many verses you will notice half-brackets (⌊ ⌋) in the text. These words were supplied by the translation team when the context contains meaning that is not explicitly stated in the original language.

We pray that *Promises from GOD'S WORD* will lead you to discover the richness of God's word and of his promises to you.

ANGER

The LORD is merciful, compassionate, patient,
and always ready to forgive.

Psalm 145:8

A gentle answer turns away rage,
but a harsh word stirs up anger.

Proverbs 15:1

A person with good sense is patient,
and it is to his credit that he overlooks an offense.

Proverbs 19:11

A fool expresses all his emotions,
but a wise person controls them.

Proverbs 29:11

An angry person stirs up a fight,
and a hothead does much wrong.

Proverbs 29:22

Be angry without sinning. Don't go to bed angry. Don't give the devil
any opportunity ⌊to work⌋.

Ephesians 4:26-27

Get rid of your bitterness, hot tempers, anger, loud quarreling, cursing, and hatred. Be kind to each other, sympathetic, forgiving each other as God has forgiven you through Christ.

Ephesians 4:31-32

Remember this, my dear brothers and sisters: Everyone should be quick to listen, slow to speak, and should not get angry easily. An angry person doesn't do what God approves of.

James 1:19-20

 # ANXIETY

I went to the LORD for help.
> He answered me and rescued me from all my fears.

Psalm 34:4

Turn your burdens over to the LORD,
> and he will take care of you.
>> He will never let the righteous person stumble.

Psalm 55:22

Trust the LORD with all your heart,
> and do not rely on your own understanding.
In all your ways acknowledge him,
> and he will make your paths smooth.

Proverbs 3:5-6

A person's anxiety will weigh him down,
  but an encouraging word makes him joyful.

Proverbs 12:25

Don't be afraid, because I am with you.
Don't be intimidated; I am your God.
  I will strengthen you.
  I will help you.
  I will support you with my victorious right hand.

Isaiah 41:10

So I tell you to stop worrying about what you will eat, drink, or wear.
Isn't life more than food and the body more than clothes?

Matthew 6:25

So don't ever worry about tomorrow. After all, tomorrow will worry
about itself. Each day has enough trouble of its own.

Matthew 6:34

Never worry about anything. But in every situation let God know what
you need in prayers and requests while giving thanks. Then God's
peace, which goes beyond anything we can imagine, will guard your
thoughts and emotions through Christ Jesus.

Philippians 4:6-7

Turn all your anxiety over to God because he cares for you.

1 Peter 5:7

❧ ARROGANCE ❧

Do not boast
⌊or⌋ let arrogance come out of your mouth
because the LORD is a God of knowledge,
and he weighs ⌊our⌋ actions.

1 Samuel 2:3

Arrogance comes,
then comes shame,
but wisdom remains with humble people.

Proverbs 11:2

Pride precedes a disaster,
and an arrogant attitude precedes a fall.

Proverbs 16:18

Praise should come from another person
and not from your own mouth,
from a stranger and not from your own lips.

Proverbs 27:2

This is what the LORD says:
Don't let wise people brag about their wisdom.
Don't let strong people brag about their strength.
Don't let rich people brag about their riches.

If they want to brag,
      they should brag that they understand and know me.
    They should brag that I, the LORD, act out of love, righteousness,
      and justice on the earth.
        This kind of bragging pleases me, declares the LORD.

Jeremiah 9:23-24

Whoever wants to be the most important person must take the last place and be a servant to everyone else.

Mark 9:35b

Because of the kindness that God has shown me, I ask you not to think of yourselves more highly than you should.

Romans 12:3a

"Whoever brags should brag about what the Lord has done." It isn't the person who makes his own recommendation who receives approval, but the person whom the Lord recommends.

2 Corinthians 10:17-18

∾ ASSERTIVENESS ∾

The LORD Almighty is my strength.
    He makes my feet like those of a deer.
      He makes me walk on the mountains.

Habakkuk 3:19

After they found out that Peter and John had no education or special training, they were surprised to see how boldly they spoke. They realized that these men had been with Jesus.

Acts 4:13

The one who loves us gives us an overwhelming victory in all these difficulties.

Romans 8:37

But he told me: "My kindness is all you need. My power is strongest when you are weak." So I will brag even more about my weaknesses in order that Christ's power will live in me.

2 Corinthians 12:9

Also pray that God will give me the right words to say. Then I will speak boldly when I reveal the mystery of the Good News.

Ephesians 6:19

I can do everything through Christ who strengthens me.

Philippians 4:13

So we can go confidently to the throne of God's kindness to receive mercy and find kindness, which will help us at the right time.

Hebrews 4:16

So we can confidently say,
   "The Lord is my helper.
      I will not be afraid.
         What can mortals do to me?"

Hebrews 13:6

~ ASSURANCE ~

⌊The LORD says,⌋
   "I will instruct you.
   I will teach you the way that you should go.
   I will advise you as my eyes watch over you."

Psalm 32:8

Let go ⌊of your concerns⌋!
   Then you will know that I am God.
      I rule the nations.
      I rule the earth.

Psalm 46:10

That's why I tell you to have faith that you have already received
whatever you pray for, and it will be yours.

Mark 11:24

My sheep respond to my voice, and I know who they are. They follow
me, and I give them eternal life. They will never be lost, and no one will

tear them away from me. My Father, who gave them to me, is greater than everyone else, and no one can tear them away from my Father.

John 10:27-29

I am convinced that nothing can ever separate us from God's love which Christ Jesus our Lord shows us. We can't be separated by death or life, by angels or rulers, by anything in the present or anything in the future, by forces or powers in the world above or in the world below, or by anything else in creation.

Romans 8:38-39

I'm convinced that God, who began this good work in you, will carry it through to completion on the day of Christ Jesus.

Philippians 1:6

God is faithful and reliable. If we confess our sins, he forgives them and cleanses us from everything we've done wrong.

1 John 1:9

We are confident that God listens to us if we ask for anything that has his approval. We know that he listens to our requests. So we know that we already have what we ask him for.

1 John 5:14-15

∞ ATTITUDES ∞

Wait with hope for the LORD.
Be strong, and let your heart be courageous.
Yes, wait with hope for the LORD.

Psalm 27:14

Love is patient. Love is kind. Love isn't jealous. It doesn't sing its own praises. It isn't arrogant. It isn't rude. It doesn't think about itself. It isn't irritable. It doesn't keep track of wrongs.

1 Corinthians 13:4-5

Don't act out of selfish ambition or be conceited. Instead, humbly think of others as being better than yourselves. Don't be concerned only about your own interests, but also be concerned about the interests of others.

Philippians 2:3-4

Brothers and sisters, I can't consider myself a winner yet. This is what I do: I don't look back, I lengthen my stride, and I run straight toward the goal to win the prize that God's heavenly call offers in Christ Jesus.

Philippians 3:13-14

I'm not saying this because I'm in any need. I've learned to be content in whatever situation I'm in.

Philippians 4:11

Since you were brought back to life with Christ, focus on the things that are above—where Christ holds the highest position. Keep your mind on things above, not on worldly things. You have died, and your life is hidden with Christ in God.

Colossians 3:1-3

Always be joyful.

1 Thessalonians 5:16

My brothers and sisters, be very happy when you are tested in different ways. You know that such testing of your faith produces endurance. Endure until your testing is over. Then you will be mature and complete, and you won't need anything.

James 1:2-4

∞ BACKSLIDING ∞

However, if my people, who are called by my name,
    will humble themselves,
    pray, search for me, and turn from their evil ways,
then I will hear ⌊their prayer⌋ from heaven, forgive their sins,
    and heal their country.

2 Chronicles 7:14

The sacrifice pleasing to God is a broken spirit.
O God, you do not despise a broken and sorrowful heart.

Psalm 51:17

Whoever covers over his sins does not prosper.
Whoever confesses and abandons them receives compassion.

Proverbs 28:13

Let wicked people abandon their ways.
Let evil people abandon their thoughts.
Let them return to the LORD,
   and he will show compassion to them.
Let them return to our God,
   because he will freely forgive them.

Isaiah 55:7

God is faithful and reliable. If we confess our sins, he forgives them
and cleanses us from everything we've done wrong.

1 John 1:9

My dear children, I'm writing this to you so that you will not sin. Yet, if
anyone does sin, we have Jesus Christ, who has God's full approval. He
speaks on our behalf when we come into the presence of the Father.

1 John 2:1

~ BELIEF ~

That's why I tell you to have faith that you have already received
whatever you pray for, and it will be yours.

Mark 11:24

However, he gave the right to become God's children to everyone who believed in him.

John 1:12

God loved the world this way: He gave his only Son so that everyone who believes in him will not die but will have eternal life.

John 3:16

Those who believe in him won't be condemned. But those who don't believe are already condemned because they don't believe in God's only Son.

John 3:18

Whoever believes in the Son has eternal life, but whoever rejects the Son will not see life. Instead, he will see God's constant anger.

John 3:36

Jesus told them, "I am the bread of life. Whoever comes to me will never become hungry, and whoever believes in me will never become thirsty."

John 6:35

They answered, "Believe in the Lord Jesus, and you . . . will be saved."

Acts 16:31

No one can please God without faith. Whoever goes to God must believe that God exists and that he rewards those who seek him.

Hebrews 11:6

∼ **BEREAVEMENT** ∼

My eyes blur from grief.
　　They fail because of my enemies.

Psalm 6:7

You have seen ⌊it⌋; yes, you have taken note of trouble and grief
　　and placed them under your control.
　　　　The victim entrusts himself to you.
You alone have been the helper of orphans.

Psalm 10:14

Have pity on me, O LORD, because I am in distress.
　　My eyes, my soul, and my body waste away from grief.

Psalm 31:9

Precious in the sight of the LORD
　　is the death of his faithful ones.

Psalm 116:15

I am drowning in tears.
　　Strengthen me as you promised.

Psalm 119:28

Even if he makes us suffer,
   he will have compassion
      in keeping with the richness of his mercy.

Lamentations 3:32

Blessed are those who mourn.
   They will be comforted.

Matthew 5:4

Don't be troubled. Believe in God, and believe in me. My Father's
house has many rooms. If that were not true, would I have told you
that I'm going to prepare a place for you? If I go to prepare a place for
you, I will come again. Then I will bring you into my presence so that
you will be where I am.

John 14:1-3

Christ means everything to me in this life, and when I die I'll have even
more. If I continue to live in this life, my work will produce more
results. I don't know which I would prefer. I find it hard to choose
between the two. I would like to leave this life and be with Christ.
That's by far the better choice.

Philippians 1:21-23

Brothers and sisters, we don't want you to be ignorant about those
who have died. We don't want you to grieve like other people who have
no hope. We believe that Jesus died and came back to life. We also

believe that, through Jesus, God will bring back those who have died.
They will come back with Jesus.

1 Thessalonians 4:13-14

He will wipe every tear from their eyes. There won't be any more
death. There won't be any grief, crying, or pain, because the first
things have disappeared.

Revelation 21:4

~ **BETRAYAL** ~

Be strong and courageous. Don't tremble! Don't be afraid of them! The
LORD your God is the one who is going with you. He won't abandon
you or leave you.

Deuteronomy 31:6

Even if my father and mother abandon me,
  the LORD will take care of me.

Psalm 27:10

Can a woman forget her nursing child?
Will she have no compassion on the child from her womb?
Although mothers may forget,
  I will not forget you.
I have engraved you on the palms of my hands.

Isaiah 49:15-16a

The mountains may move, and the hills may shake,
   but my kindness will never depart from you.
      My promise of peace will never change,
         says the LORD, who has compassion on you.

Isaiah 54:10

If we endure, we will rule with him.
If we disown him, he will disown us.
If we are unfaithful, he remains faithful
   because he cannot be untrue to himself.

2 Timothy 2:12-13

❧ BIBLE ❧

Never stop reciting these teachings. You must think about them night and day so that you will faithfully do everything written in them. Only then will you prosper and succeed.

Joshua 1:8

How can a young person keep his life pure?
   ⌊He can do it⌋ by holding on to your word.
I wholeheartedly searched for you.
   Do not let me wander away from your commandments.
I have treasured your promise in my heart
   so that I may not sin against you.

Psalm 119:9-11

O LORD, your word is established in heaven forever.

Psalm 119:89

Your word is a lamp for my feet
   and a light for my path.

Psalm 119:105

I can guarantee this truth: Until the earth and the heavens disappear, neither a period nor a comma will disappear from Moses' Teachings before everything has come true.

Matthew 5:18

Everything written long ago was written to teach us so that we would have confidence through the endurance and encouragement which the Scriptures give us.

Romans 15:4

Here is another reason why we never stop thanking God: When you received God's word from us, you realized it wasn't the word of humans. Instead, you accepted it for what it really is—the word of God. This word is at work in you believers.

1 Thessalonians 2:13

Every Scripture passage is inspired by God. All of them are useful for teaching, pointing out errors, correcting people, and training them for a life that has God's approval. They equip God's servants so that they are completely prepared to do good things.

2 Timothy 3:16-17

God's word is living and active. It is sharper than any two-edged sword and cuts as deep as the place where soul and spirit meet, the place where joints and marrow meet. God's word judges a person's thoughts and intentions.

Hebrews 4:12

First, you must understand this: No prophecy in Scripture is a matter of one's own interpretation. No prophecy ever originated from humans. Instead, it was given by the Holy Spirit as humans spoke under God's direction.

2 Peter 1:20-21

❧ BITTERNESS ❧

So if you are offering your gift at the altar and remember there that another believer has something against you, leave your gift at the altar. First go away and make peace with that person. Then come back and offer your gift.

Matthew 5:23-24

So if the Son sets you free, you will be absolutely free.

John 8:36

Love is patient. Love is kind. Love isn't jealous. It doesn't sing its own praises. It isn't arrogant. It isn't rude. It doesn't think about itself. It isn't irritable. It doesn't keep track of wrongs. It isn't happy when injustice is done, but it is happy with the truth.

1 Corinthians 13:4-6

Whoever is a believer in Christ is a new creation. The old way of living has disappeared. A new way of living has come into existence.

2 Corinthians 5:17

Get rid of your bitterness, hot tempers, anger, loud quarreling, cursing, and hatred. Be kind to each other, sympathetic, forgiving each other as God has forgiven you through Christ.

Ephesians 4:31-32

Put up with each other, and forgive each other if anyone has a complaint. Forgive as the Lord forgave you.

Colossians 3:13

Try to live peacefully with everyone, and try to live holy lives, because if you don't, you will not see the Lord. Make sure that everyone has kindness from God so that bitterness doesn't take root and grow up to cause trouble that corrupts many of you.

Hebrews 12:14-15

❧ BLESSING ❧

I will make you a great nation,
I will bless you.

I will make your name great,
> and you will be a blessing.

Genesis 12:2

Today I'm giving you the choice of a blessing or a curse. You'll be
blessed if you obey the commands of the LORD your God that I'm
giving you today.

Deuteronomy 11:26-27

Your kindness is so great!
> You reserve it for those who fear you.

Psalm 31:19a

May God bless us,
> and may all the ends of the earth worship him.

Psalm 67:7

Blessed is the person who trusts the LORD.
> The LORD will be his confidence.

Jeremiah 17:7

Besides, God will give you his constantly overflowing kindness. Then,
when you always have everything you need, you can do more and
more good things.

2 Corinthians 9:8

Praise the God and Father of our Lord Jesus Christ! Through Christ, God has blessed us with every spiritual blessing that heaven has to offer.

Ephesians 1:3

Don't pay people back with evil for the evil they do to you, or ridicule those who ridicule you. Instead, bless them, because you were called to inherit a blessing.

1 Peter 3:9

∽ **BOLDNESS** ∽

Wait with hope for the LORD.
Be strong, and let your heart be courageous.
Yes, wait with hope for the LORD.

Psalm 27:14

The LORD will be your confidence.
He will keep your foot from getting caught.

Proverbs 3:26

Don't be afraid, because I am with you.
Don't be intimidated; I am your God.
    I will strengthen you.
    I will help you.
    I will support you with my victorious right hand.

Isaiah 41:10

You won't ⌞succeed⌟ by might or by power, but by my Spirit, says the LORD of Armies.

Zechariah 4:6b

The one who loves us gives us an overwhelming victory in all these difficulties. I am convinced that nothing can ever separate us from God's love which Christ Jesus our Lord shows us. We can't be separated by death or life, by angels or rulers, by anything in the present or anything in the future, by forces or powers in the world above or in the world below, or by anything else in creation.

Romans 8:37-39

I eagerly expect and hope that I will have nothing to be ashamed of. I will speak very boldly and honor Christ in my body, now as always, whether I live or die.

Philippians 1:20

I can do everything through Christ who strengthens me.

Philippians 4:13

So we can go confidently to the throne of God's kindness to receive mercy and find kindness, which will help us at the right time.

Hebrews 4:16

So we can confidently say,
  "The Lord is my helper.

I will not be afraid.
What can mortals do to me?"

Hebrews 13:6

Dear children, you belong to God. So you have won the victory over these people, because the one who is in you is greater than the one who is in the world.

1 John 4:4

❧ BOREDOM ❧

You make the path of life known to me.
Complete joy is in your presence.
Pleasures are by your side forever.

Psalm 16:11

Then our mouths were filled with laughter
and our tongues with joyful songs.
Then the nations said,
"The LORD has done spectacular things for them."

Psalm 126:2

These people won't give much thought to their brief lives because God keeps them occupied with the joy in their hearts.

Ecclesiastes 5:20

We want each of you to prove that you're working hard so that you will
remain confident until the end. Then, instead of being lazy, you will
imitate those who are receiving the promises through faith and
patience.

Hebrews 6:11-12

✺ BRAVERY ✺

Don't be afraid of them, because the LORD your God is with you. He is
a great and awe-inspiring God.

Deuteronomy 7:21

Don't be afraid. We have more forces on our side than they have on
theirs.

2 Kings 6:16b

You won't fight this battle. ⌊Instead,⌋ take your position, stand still, and
see the victory of the LORD for you, Judah and Jerusalem. Don't be
frightened or terrified. Tomorrow go out to face them. The LORD is
with you.

2 Chronicles 20:17

With you I can attack a line of soldiers.
With my God I can break through barricades.

Psalm 18:29

God arms me with strength
   and makes my way perfect.

Psalm 18:32

The LORD is my strength and my shield.
My heart trusted him, so I received help.
My heart is triumphant; I give thanks to him with my song.

Psalm 28:7

When I am in trouble, I call out to you
   because you answer me.

Psalm 86:7

I'm asking God to give you a gift from the wealth of his glory. I pray
that he would give you inner strength and power through his Spirit.

Ephesians 3:16

Finally, receive your power from the Lord and from his mighty
strength. . . . For this reason, take up all the armor that God supplies.
Then you will be able to take a stand during these evil days. Once you
have overcome all obstacles, you will be able to stand your ground.

Ephesians 6:10, 13

Dear children, you belong to God. So you have won the victory over
these people, because the one who is in you is greater than the one
who is in the world.

1 John 4:4

❧ CARE OF GOD ❧

You gave me life and mercy.
  Your watchfulness has preserved my spirit.

Job 10:12

What is a mortal that you remember him
  or the Son of Man that you take care of him?

Psalm 8:4

He is our God
  and we are the people in his care,
    the flock that he leads.

Psalm 95:7a

O LORD, you have examined me, and you know me.
  You alone know when I sit down and when I get up.
  You read my thoughts from far away. . . .
  You are all around me—in front of me and in back of me.
  You lay your hand on me.

Psalm 139:1-2, 5

How precious are your thoughts concerning me, O God!
How vast in number they are!
  If I try to count them,

    there would be more of them than there are grains of sand.
      When I wake up, I am still with you.

Psalm 139:17-18

So I tell you to stop worrying about what you will eat, drink, or wear.
Isn't life more than food and the body more than clothes?
    Look at the birds. They don't plant, harvest, or gather the harvest
into barns. Yet, your heavenly Father feeds them. Aren't you worth
more than they?

Matthew 6:25-26

Don't ever worry and say, "What are we going to eat?" or "What are we
going to drink?" or "What are we going to wear?" Everyone is
concerned about these things, and your heavenly Father certainly
knows you need all of them. But first, be concerned about his kingdom
and what has his approval. Then all these things will be provided
for you.

Matthew 6:31-33

My God will richly fill your every need in a glorious way through
Christ Jesus.

Philippians 4:19

Turn all your anxiety over to God because he cares for you.

1 Peter 5:7

❧ CATASTROPHE ❧

On the day when I faced disaster, they confronted me,
    but the LORD came to my defense.

Psalm 18:18

I waited patiently for the LORD.
    He turned to me and heard my cry for help.
    He pulled me out of a horrible pit,
        out of the mud and clay.
    He set my feet on a rock
        and made my steps secure.
    He placed a new song in my mouth,
        a song of praise to our God.
            Many will see this and worship.
            They will trust the LORD.

Psalm 40:1-3

During times of trouble I called on the LORD.
    The LORD answered me ⌊and⌋ set me free ⌊from all of them⌋.
The LORD is on my side.
    I am not afraid.
        What can mortals do to me?

Psalm 118:5-6

Even though I walk into the middle of trouble,
   you guard my life against the anger of my enemies.
  You stretch out your hand,
    and your right hand saves me.

Psalm 138:7

But whoever listens to me will live without worry
  and will be free from the dread of disaster.

Proverbs 1:33

When you go through the sea, I am with you.
When you go through rivers, they will not sweep you away.
When you walk through fire, you will not be burned,
  and the flames will not harm you.

Isaiah 43:2

  The people ransomed by the LORD will return.
    They will come to Zion singing with joy.
      Everlasting happiness will be on their heads ⌊as a crown⌋.
     They will be glad and joyful.
     They will have no sorrow or grief.

Isaiah 51:11

The LORD is good.
  ⌊He is⌋ a fortress in the day of trouble.
  He knows those who seek shelter in him.

Nahum 1:7

We know that all things work together for the good of those who love God—those whom he has called according to his plan.

Romans 8:28

Praise the God and Father of our Lord Jesus Christ! He is the Father who is compassionate and the God who gives comfort. He comforts us whenever we suffer. That is why whenever other people suffer, we are able to comfort them by using the same comfort we have received from God.

2 Corinthians 1:3-4

In every way we're troubled, but we aren't crushed by our troubles. We're frustrated, but we don't give up. We're persecuted, but we're not abandoned. We're captured, but we're not killed.

2 Corinthians 4:8-9

Never worry about anything. But in every situation let God know what you need in prayers and requests while giving thanks. Then God's peace, which goes beyond anything we can imagine, will guard your thoughts and emotions through Christ Jesus.

Philippians 4:6-7

∞ **CHANGE** ∞

O LORD, your word is established in heaven forever.
Your faithfulness endures throughout every generation.
You set the earth in place, and it continues to stand.

Psalm 119:89-90

I am convinced that nothing can ever separate us from God's love which Christ Jesus our Lord shows us. We can't be separated by death or life, by angels or rulers, by anything in the present or anything in the future, by forces or powers in the world above or in the world below, or by anything else in creation.

Romans 8:38-39

Don't become like the people of this world. Instead, change the way you think. Then you will always be able to determine what God really wants—what is good, pleasing, and perfect.

Romans 12:2

As all of us reflect the Lord's glory with faces that are not covered with veils, we are being changed into his image with ever-increasing glory. This comes from the Lord, who is the Spirit.

2 Corinthians 3:18

Whoever is a believer in Christ is a new creation. The old way of living has disappeared. A new way of living has come into existence.

2 Corinthians 5:17

Jesus Christ is the same yesterday, today, and forever.

Hebrews 13:8

❧ CHEATING ❧

If you sell anything to your neighbor or buy anything from him, don't take advantage of him.

Leviticus 25:14

Never take advantage of each other. Fear your God, because I am the LORD your God.

Leviticus 25:17

Whoever can be trusted with very little can also be trusted with a lot. Whoever is dishonest with very little is dishonest with a lot. Therefore, if you can't be trusted with wealth that is often used dishonestly, who will trust you with wealth that is real?

Luke 16:10-11

The commandments, "Never commit adultery; never murder; never steal; never have wrong desires," and every other commandment are summed up in this statement: "Love your neighbor as you love yourself."

Romans 13:9

∞ CHILDREN ∞

Children are an inheritance from the LORD.
They are a reward from him.
The children born to a man when he is young
are like arrows in the hand of a warrior.
Blessed is the man who has filled his quiver with them.
He will not be put to shame
when he speaks with his enemies in the city gate.

Psalm 127:3-5

A wise son listens to his father's discipline,
but a mocker does not listen to reprimands.

Proverbs 13:1

Train a child in the way he should go,
and even when he is old he will not turn away from it.

Proverbs 22:6

Correct your son, and he will give you peace of mind.
He will bring delight to your soul.

Proverbs 29:17

All your children will be taught by the LORD,
and your children will have unlimited peace.

Isaiah 54:13

When Jesus saw this, he became irritated. He told them, "Don't stop the children from coming to me. Children like these are part of the kingdom of God. I can guarantee this truth: Whoever doesn't receive the kingdom of God as a little child receives it will never enter it." Jesus put his arms around the children and blessed them by placing his hands on them.

Mark 10:14-16

Children, obey your parents because you are Christians. This is the right thing to do. "Honor your father and mother that everything may go well for you, and you may have a long life on earth." This is an important commandment with a promise.

Ephesians 6:1-3

Children, always obey your parents. This is pleasing to the Lord. Fathers, don't make your children resentful, or they will become discouraged.

Colossians 3:20-21

✎ CHURCH ✎

See how good and pleasant it is
    when brothers and sisters live together in harmony!

Psalm 133:1

Our bodies have many parts, but these parts don't all do the same thing. In the same way, even though we are many individuals, Christ makes us one body and individuals who are connected to each other.

Romans 12:4-5

God's purpose was that the body should not be divided but rather that all of its parts should feel the same concern for each other. If one part of the body suffers, all the other parts share its suffering. If one part is praised, all the others share in its happiness.
You are Christ's body and each of you is an individual part of it.

1 Corinthians 12:25-27

There are neither Jews nor Greeks, slaves nor free people, males nor females. You are all the same in Christ Jesus.

Galatians 3:28

I, a prisoner in the Lord, encourage you to live the kind of life which proves that God has called you. Be humble and gentle in every way. Be patient with each other and lovingly accept each other. Through the peace that ties you together, do your best to maintain the unity that the Spirit gives. There is one body and one Spirit. In the same way you were called to share one hope. There is one Lord, one faith, one baptism, one God and Father of all, who is over everything, through everything, and in everything.

Ephesians 4:1-6

He also gave apostles, prophets, missionaries, as well as pastors and teachers as gifts ₍to his church₎. Their purpose is to prepare God's people, to serve, and to build up the body of Christ. This is to continue until all of us are united in our faith and in our knowledge about God's Son, until we become mature, until we measure up to Christ, who is the standard.

Ephesians 4:11-13

He is also the head of the church, which is his body.
He is the beginning,
    the first to come back to life
        so that he would have first place in everything.

Colossians 1:18

We must also consider how to encourage each other to show love and to do good things. We should not stop gathering together with other believers, as some of you are doing. Instead, we must continue to encourage each other even more as we see the day of the Lord coming.

Hebrews 10:24-25

Obey your leaders, and accept their authority. They take care of you because they are responsible for you. Obey them so that they may do this work joyfully and not complain about you. (Causing them to complain would not be to your advantage.)

Hebrews 13:17

❧ COMFORT ❧

Even though I walk through the dark valley of death,
    because you are with me, I fear no harm.
        Your rod and your staff give me courage.

Psalm 23:4

Be strong, all who wait with hope for the LORD,
    and let your heart be courageous.

Psalm 31:24

But from everlasting to everlasting,
    the LORD's mercy is on those who fear him.
        His righteousness belongs
            to their children and grandchildren.

Psalm 103:17

This is my comfort in my misery:
    Your promise gave me a new life.

Psalm 119:50

Let your mercy comfort me
    as you promised.

Psalm 119:76

Don't be afraid, because I am with you.
Don't be intimidated; I am your God.

I will strengthen you.
I will help you.
I will support you with my victorious right hand.

Isaiah 41:10

Sing with joy, you heavens!
Rejoice, you earth!
Break into shouts of joy, you mountains!
  The LORD has comforted his people
    and will have compassion on his humble people.

Isaiah 49:13

Come to me, all who are tired from carrying heavy loads, and I will
give you rest.

Matthew 11:28

I'm leaving you peace. I'm giving you my peace. I don't give you the
kind of peace that the world gives. So don't be troubled or cowardly.

John 14:27

Praise the God and Father of our Lord Jesus Christ! He is the Father
who is compassionate and the God who gives comfort. He comforts us
whenever we suffer. That is why whenever other people suffer, we are
able to comfort them by using the same comfort we have received
from God.

2 Corinthians 1:3-4

We can't allow ourselves to get tired of living the right way. Certainly, each of us will receive ⌊everlasting life⌋ at the proper time, if we don't give up.

Galatians 6:9

God our Father loved us and by his kindness gave us everlasting encouragement and good hope. Together with our Lord Jesus Christ, may he encourage and strengthen you to do and say everything that is good.

2 Thessalonians 2:16-17

~ COMPLAINTS ~

Morning, noon, and night I complain and groan,
   and he listens to my voice.

Psalm 55:17

I pour out my complaints in his presence
   and tell him my troubles.

Psalm 142:2

Do everything without complaining or arguing. Then you will be blameless and innocent. You will be God's children without any faults among people who are crooked and corrupt. You will shine like stars among them in the world.

Philippians 2:14-15

I'm not saying this because I'm in any need. I've learned to be content in whatever situation I'm in. I know how to live in poverty or prosperity. No matter what the situation, I've learned the secret of how to live when I'm full or when I'm hungry, when I have too much or when I have too little. I can do everything through Christ who strengthens me.

Philippians 4:11-13

Think about Jesus, who endured opposition from sinners, so that you don't become tired and give up.
    You struggle against sin, but your struggles haven't killed you.

Hebrews 12:3-4

All of us make a lot of mistakes. If someone doesn't make any mistakes when he speaks, he would be perfect. He would be able to control everything he does.

James 3:2

Welcome each other as guests without complaining.

1 Peter 4:9

✎ CONFIDENCE ✎

The LORD is my light and my salvation.
    Who is there to fear?

The LORD is my life's fortress.
  Who is there to be afraid of?

Psalm 27:1

It is better to depend on the LORD
  than to trust mortals.

Psalm 118:8

In the fear of the LORD there is strong confidence,
  and his children will have a place of refuge.

Proverbs 14:26

You won't ⌊succeed⌋ by might or by power, but by my Spirit, says the
LORD of Armies.

Zechariah 4:6b

But he told me: "My kindness is all you need. My power is strongest
when you are weak." So I will brag even more about my weaknesses in
order that Christ's power will live in me.

2 Corinthians 12:9

I'm asking God to give you a gift from the wealth of his glory. I pray
that he would give you inner strength and power through his Spirit.

Ephesians 3:16

I'm convinced that God, who began this good work in you, will carry it
through to completion on the day of Christ Jesus.

Philippians 1:6

So we can confidently say,
   " The Lord is my helper.
      I will not be afraid.
         What can mortals do to me?"

Hebrews 13:

Now, dear children, live in Christ. Then, when he appears we will have confidence, and when he comes we won't turn from him in shame.

1 John 2:2

CONTENTMENT

Naked I came from my mother,
   and naked I will return.
The LORD has given,
   and the LORD has taken away!
May the name of the LORD be praised.

Job 1:2

You are my Lord. Without you, I have nothing good.

Psalm 16:

Be happy with the LORD,
   and he will give you the desires of your heart.

Psalm 37:

Turn my eyes away from worthless things.
Give me a new life in your ways.

Psalm 119:37

Every day is a terrible day for a miserable person,
 but a cheerful heart has a continual feast.

Proverbs 15:15

Jesus told them, "I am the bread of life. Whoever comes to me will never become hungry, and whoever believes in me will never become thirsty."

John 6:35

Never worry about anything. But in every situation let God know what you need in prayers and requests while giving thanks. Then God's peace, which goes beyond anything we can imagine, will guard your thoughts and emotions through Christ Jesus.

Philippians 4:6-7

I'm not saying this because I'm in any need. I've learned to be content in whatever situation I'm in. I know how to live in poverty or prosperity. No matter what the situation, I've learned the secret of how to live when I'm full or when I'm hungry, when I have too much or when I have too little. I can do everything through Christ who strengthens me.

Philippians 4:11-13

My God will richly fill your every need in a glorious way through Christ Jesus.

Philippians 4:19

A godly life brings huge profits to people who are content with what they have. We didn't bring anything into the world, and we can't take anything out of it.

1 Timothy 6:6-7

Don't love money. Be happy with what you have because God has said, "I will never abandon you or leave you."

Hebrews 13:5

God's divine power has given us everything we need for life and for godliness. This power was given to us through knowledge of the one who called us by his own glory and integrity.

2 Peter 1:3

❧ COURAGE ❧

I have commanded you, "Be strong and courageous! Don't tremble or be terrified, because the LORD your God is with you wherever you go."

Joshua 1:9

The LORD is my light and my salvation.
  Who is there to fear?

The LORD is my life's fortress.
   Who is there to be afraid of?

Psalm 27:1

Wait with hope for the LORD.
Be strong, and let your heart be courageous.
Yes, wait with hope for the LORD.

Psalm 27:14

He gives strength to those who grow tired
   and increases the strength of those who are weak.

Isaiah 40:29

Don't be afraid, because I am with you.
Don't be intimidated; I am your God.
   I will strengthen you.
   I will help you.
   I will support you with my victorious right hand.

Isaiah 41:10

The LORD created Jacob and formed Israel. Now, this is what the LORD says:
   Do not be afraid, because I have reclaimed you.
      I have called you by name; you are mine.
   When you go through the sea, I am with you.
   When you go through rivers, they will not sweep you away.

When you walk through fire, you will not be burned,
and the flames will not harm you.

Isaiah 43:1-2

"Don't be afraid of people. I am with you, and I will rescue you,"
declares the LORD.

Jeremiah 1:8

But he told me: "My kindness is all you need. My power is strongest
when you are weak." So I will brag even more about my weaknesses in
order that Christ's power will live in me. Therefore, I accept weakness,
mistreatment, hardship, persecution, and difficulties suffered for
Christ. It's clear that when I'm weak, I'm strong.

2 Corinthians 12:9-10

I can do everything through Christ who strengthens me.

Philippians 4:13

God didn't give us a cowardly spirit but a spirit of power, love, and
good judgment.

2 Timothy 1:7

Dear friends, don't be surprised by the fiery troubles that are coming
in order to test you. Don't feel as though something strange is
happening to you, but be happy as you share Christ's sufferings. Then
you will also be full of joy when he appears again in his glory.

1 Peter 4:12-13

CRISIS

The eternal God is your shelter,
  and his everlasting arms support you.
He will force your enemies out of your way
  and tell you to destroy them.

Deuteronomy 33:27

I will rejoice and be glad because of your mercy.
  You have seen my misery.
  You have known the troubles in my soul.

Psalm 31:7

He pulled me out of a horrible pit,
  out of the mud and clay.
He set my feet on a rock
  and made my steps secure.

Psalm 40:2

God is our refuge and strength,
  an ever-present help in times of trouble.

Psalm 46:1

The name of the LORD is a strong tower.
  A righteous person runs to it and is safe.

Proverbs 18:10

When you go through the sea, I am with you.
When you go through rivers, they will not sweep you away.
When you walk through fire, you will not be burned,
    and the flames will not harm you.

Isaiah 43:2

Don't be troubled. Believe in God.

John 14:1a

We know that all things work together for the good of those who love
God—those whom he has called according to his plan.

Romans 8:28

Praise the God and Father of our Lord Jesus Christ! He is the Father
who is compassionate and the God who gives comfort. He comforts us
whenever we suffer. That is why whenever other people suffer, we are
able to comfort them by using the same comfort we have received
from God.

2 Corinthians 1:3-4

In every way we're troubled, but we aren't crushed by our troubles.
We're frustrated, but we don't give up. We're persecuted, but we're not
abandoned. We're captured, but we're not killed.

2 Corinthians 4:8-9

∼ CRITICISM ∼

Sin is unavoidable when there is much talk,
   but whoever seals his lips is wise.

Proverbs 10:19

The person who is truly wise is called understanding,
   and speaking sweetly helps others learn.

Proverbs 16:21

⌊Like⌋ golden apples in silver settings,
   ⌊so⌋ is a word spoken at the right time.

Proverbs 25:11

Blessed are you when people insult you,
   persecute you,
      lie, and say all kinds of evil things about you because of me.
Rejoice and be glad because you have a great reward in heaven!
   The prophets who lived before you were persecuted in these ways.
Matthew 5:11-12

Everything you say should be kind and well thought out so that you
know how to answer everyone.

Colossians 4:6

Don't let anyone look down on you for being young. Instead, make your speech, behavior, love, faith, and purity an example for other believers.

1 Timothy 4:12

However, the wisdom that comes from above is first of all pure. Then it is peaceful, gentle, obedient, filled with mercy and good deeds, impartial, and sincere.

James 3:17

✎ DANGER ✎

The LORD's beloved people will live securely with him.
    The LORD will shelter them all day long.

Deuteronomy 33:12b

You will feel confident because there's hope,
    and you will look around and rest in safety.

Job 11:18

I fall asleep in peace the moment I lie down
    because you alone, O LORD, enable me to live securely.

Psalm 4:8

He hides me in his shelter when there is trouble.
He keeps me hidden in his tent.
He sets me high on a rock.

Psalm 27:5

You have been my refuge,
   a tower of strength against the enemy.
I would like to be a guest in your tent forever
   and to take refuge under the protection of your wings.

Psalm 61:3-4

Whoever lives under the shelter of the Most High
   will remain in the shadow of the Almighty.
I will say to the LORD,
   "⌊You are⌋ my refuge and my fortress, my God in whom I trust."

Psalm 91:1-2

The name of the LORD is a strong tower.
   A righteous person runs to it and is safe.

Proverbs 18:10

Sensible people foresee trouble and hide ⌊from it⌋,
   but gullible people go ahead and suffer ⌊the consequence⌋.

Proverbs 22:3

You have been a refuge for the poor,
    a refuge for the needy in their distress,
    a shelter from the rain, and shade from the heat.

Isaiah 25:4a

But the Lord is faithful and will strengthen you and protect you against the evil one.

2 Thessalonians 3:3

Dear children, you belong to God. So you have won the victory over these people, because the one who is in you is greater than the one who is in the world.

1 John 4:4

❧ DEATH ❧

Even though I walk through the dark valley of death,
    because you are with me, I fear no harm.
        Your rod and your staff give me courage.

Psalm 23:4

Blessed are those who mourn.
    They will be comforted.

Matthew 5:4

Jesus said to her, "I am the one who brings people back to life, and I am life itself. Those who believe in me will live even if they die.

Everyone who lives and believes in me will never die. Do you believe that?"

John 11:25-26

My Father's house has many rooms. If that were not true, would I have told you that I'm going to prepare a place for you? If I go to prepare a place for you, I will come again. Then I will bring you into my presence so that you will be where I am.

John 14:2-3

The reward for sin is death, but the gift that God freely gives is everlasting life found in Christ Jesus our Lord.

Romans 6:23

I am convinced that nothing can ever separate us from God's love which Christ Jesus our Lord shows us. We can't be separated by death or life, by angels or rulers, by anything in the present or anything in the future, by forces or powers in the world above or in the world below, or by anything else in creation.

Romans 8:38-39

That is why we are not discouraged. Though outwardly we are wearing out, inwardly we are renewed day by day.

2 Corinthians 4:16

So we are always confident. We know that as long as we are living in these bodies, we are living away from the Lord. Indeed, our lives are guided by faith, not by sight. We are confident and prefer to live away from this body and to live with the Lord.

2 Corinthians 5:6-8

This is the testimony: God has given us eternal life, and this life is found in his Son.

1 John 5:11

✒ DECISIONS ✒

⌊The LORD says,⌋
"I will instruct you.
I will teach you the way that you should go.
I will advise you as my eyes watch over you.

Psalm 32:8

A person's steps are directed by the LORD,
and the LORD delights in his way.

Psalm 37:23

Trust the LORD with all your heart,
and do not rely on your own understanding.
In all your ways acknowledge him,
and he will make your paths smooth.

Proverbs 3:5-6

A person may plan his own journey,
   but the LORD directs his steps.

Proverbs 16:9

You will hear a voice behind you saying, "This is the way. Follow it,
whether it turns to the right or to the left."

Isaiah 30:21

O LORD, I know that the way humans act is not under their control.
   Humans do not direct their steps as they walk.

Jeremiah 10:23

I know the plans that I have for you, declares the LORD. They are plans
for peace and not disaster, plans to give you a future filled with hope.

Jeremiah 29:11

Call to me, and I will answer you. I will tell you great and mysterious
things that you do not know.

Jeremiah 33:3

❧ DEFIANCE ❧

Is the LORD as delighted with burnt offerings and sacrifices
   as he would be with your obedience?
To follow instructions is better than to sacrifice.
To obey is better than sacrificing the fat of rams.
   The sin of black magic is rebellion.

Wickedness and idolatry are arrogance.
Because you rejected the word of the LORD,
  he rejects you as king.

1 Samuel 15:22-23

A person who will not bend after many warnings
  will suddenly be broken beyond repair.

Proverbs 29:1

Tear your hearts, not your clothes.
  Return to the LORD your God.
    He is merciful and compassionate,
      patient, and always ready to forgive
        and to change his plans about disaster.

Joel 2:13

Therefore, everyone who hears what I say and obeys it will be like a
wise person who built a house on rock.

Matthew 7:24

Place yourselves under each other's authority out of respect for Christ.

Ephesians 5:21

Obey your leaders, and accept their authority. They take care of you
because they are responsible for you. Obey them so that they may do
this work joyfully and not complain about you. (Causing them to
complain would not be to your advantage.)

Hebrews 13:17

So place yourselves under God's authority. Resist the devil, and he will run away from you.

James 4:7

~ DEPRESSION ~

His anger lasts only a moment.
His favor lasts a lifetime.
  Weeping may last for the night,
    but there is a song of joy in the morning.

Psalm 30:5b

He is the healer of the brokenhearted.
He is the one who bandages their wounds.

Psalm 147:3

Trust the LORD with all your heart,
  and do not rely on your own understanding.
In all your ways acknowledge him,
  and he will make your paths smooth.

Proverbs 3:5-6

With perfect peace you will protect
    those whose minds cannot be changed,
  because they trust you.

Isaiah 26:3

Yet, the strength of those who wait with hope in the LORD
   will be renewed.
     They will soar on wings like eagles.
      They will run and won't become weary.
      They will walk and won't grow tired.

Isaiah 40:31

The people ransomed by the LORD will return.
   They will come to Zion singing with joy.
     Everlasting happiness will be on their heads ⌊as a crown⌋.
     They will be glad and joyful.
     They will have no sorrow or grief.

Isaiah 51:11

He certainly has taken upon himself our suffering
   and carried our sorrows,
     but we thought that God had wounded him,
      beat him, and punished him.
He was wounded for our rebellious acts.
He was crushed for our sins.
   He was punished so that we could have peace,
   and we received healing from his wounds.

Isaiah 53:4-5

Praise the God and Father of our Lord Jesus Christ! He is the Father
who is compassionate and the God who gives comfort. He comforts us

whenever we suffer. That is why whenever other people suffer, we are able to comfort them by using the same comfort we have received from God.

2 Corinthians 1:3-4

In every way we're troubled, but we aren't crushed by our troubles. We're frustrated, but we don't give up. We're persecuted, but we're not abandoned. We're captured, but we're not killed.

2 Corinthians 4:8-9

Be humbled by God's power so that when the right time comes he will honor you.

Turn all your anxiety over to God because he cares for you.

1 Peter 5:6-7

➣ **DETERMINATION** ➣

However, be careful, and watch yourselves closely so that you don't forget the things which you have seen with your own eyes. Don't let them fade from your memory as long as you live. Teach them to your children and grandchildren.

Deuteronomy 4:9

I have treasured your promise in my heart
    so that I may not sin against you.

Psalm 119:11

The Almighty LORD helps me.
That is why I will not be ashamed.
I have set my face like a flint.
I know that I will not be put to shame.

Isaiah 50:7

So, then, brothers and sisters, don't let anyone move you off the foundation ⌊of your faith⌋. Always excel in the work you do for the Lord. You know that the hard work you do for the Lord is not pointless.

1 Corinthians 15:58

We can't allow ourselves to get tired of living the right way. Certainly, each of us will receive ⌊everlasting life⌋ at the proper time, if we don't give up.

Galatians 6:9

Blessed are those who endure when they are tested. When they pass the test, they will receive the crown of life that God has promised to those who love him.

James 1:12

So place yourselves under God's authority. Resist the devil, and he will run away from you.

James 4:7

Keep your mind clear, and be alert. Your opponent the devil is prowling around like a roaring lion as he looks for someone to devour.

Be firm in the faith and resist him, knowing that other believers throughout the world are going through the same kind of suffering.

1 Peter 5:8-9

❧ DEVOTION ❧

I am the LORD your God, who brought you out of slavery in Egypt. Never have any other god.

Exodus 20:2-3

Love the LORD your God with all your heart, with all your soul, and with all your strength.

Deuteronomy 6:5

But if you don't want to serve the LORD, then choose today whom you will serve. . . . My family and I will still serve the LORD.

Joshua 24:15

Protect me, because I am faithful ⌊to you⌋.
Save your servant who trusts you. You are my God.

Psalm 86:2

No one can serve two masters. He will hate the first master and love the second, or he will be devoted to the first and despise the second. You cannot serve God and wealth.

Matthew 6:24

Be devoted to each other like a loving family. Excel in showing respect for each other. Don't be lazy in showing your devotion. Use your energy to serve the Lord. Be happy in your confidence, be patient in trouble, and pray continually.

Romans 12:10-12

However, I'm afraid that as the snake deceived Eve by its tricks, so your minds may somehow be lured away from your sincere and pure devotion to Christ.

2 Corinthians 11:3

❧ DISAPPOINTMENT ❧

Wait with hope for the LORD.
Be strong, and let your heart be courageous.
Yes, wait with hope for the LORD.

Psalm 27:14

The LORD is near to everyone who prays to him,
    to every faithful person who prays to him.

Psalm 145:18

"The mountains may move, and the hills may shake,
    but my kindness will never depart from you.
        My promise of peace will never change,"
            says the LORD, who has compassion on you.

Isaiah 54:10

I will not leave you all alone. I will come back to you.

John 14:18

But that's not all. We also brag when we are suffering. We know that suffering creates endurance, endurance creates character, and character creates confidence. We're not ashamed to have this confidence, because God's love has been poured into our hearts by the Holy Spirit, who has been given to us.

Romans 5:3-5

We know that all things work together for the good of those who love God—those whom he has called according to his plan.

Romans 8:28

Whatever happens, give thanks, because it is God's will in Christ Jesus that you do this.

1 Thessalonians 5:18

You don't have the things you want, because you don't pray for them. When you pray for things, you don't get them because you want them for the wrong reason—for your own pleasure.

James 4:2b-3

❧ DISCOURAGEMENT ❧

Be strong, all who wait with hope for the LORD,
   and let your heart be courageous.

Psalm 31:24

Why are you discouraged, my soul?
Why are you so restless?
   Put your hope in God,
      because I will still praise him.
         He is my savior and my God.

Psalm 43:5

You have made me endure many terrible troubles.
You restore me to life again.
You bring me back from the depths of the earth.

Psalm 71:20

Hallelujah!
Give thanks to the LORD because he is good,
   because his mercy endures forever.
Who can speak about all the mighty things the LORD has done?
Who can announce all the things for which he is worthy of praise?

Psalm 106:1-2

When I called, you answered me.
    You made me bold by strengthening my soul.

Psalm 138:3

The LORD will do everything for me.
O LORD, your mercy endures forever.
Do not let go of what your hands have made.

Psalm 138:8

I know the plans that I have for you, declares the LORD. They are plans
for peace and not disaster, plans to give you a future filled with hope.

Jeremiah 29:11

At the same time the Spirit also helps us in our weakness, because we
don't know how to pray for what we need. But the Spirit intercedes
along with our groans that cannot be expressed in words. The one who
searches our hearts knows what the Spirit has in mind. The Spirit
intercedes for God's people the way God wants him to.

Romans 8:26-27

God is fair. He won't forget what you've done or the love you've shown
for him.

Hebrews 6:10a

✎ DISGRACE ✎

How terrible it will be for me if I'm guilty!
　　Even if I'm righteous, I dare not lift up my head.
I am filled with disgrace
　　while I look on my misery.

Job 10:15

I made my sins known to you, and I did not cover up my guilt.
I decided to confess them to you, O LORD.
　　Then you forgave all my sins.

Psalm 32:5

As far as the east is from the west—
　　that is how far he has removed our rebellious acts from himself.

Psalm 103:12

Poverty and shame come to a person who ignores discipline,
　　but whoever pays attention
　　　　to constructive criticism will be honored.

Proverbs 13:18

If you forgive the failures of others, your heavenly Father will also
forgive you. But if you don't forgive others, your Father will not forgive
your failures.

Matthew 6:14-15

So those who are believers in Christ Jesus can no longer be condemned.

Romans 8:1

If you suffer for being a Christian, don't feel ashamed, but praise God for being called that name.

1 Peter 4:16

God is faithful and reliable. If we confess our sins, he forgives them and cleanses us from everything we've done wrong.

1 John 1:9

❧ DOUBTS ❧

Jesus said to them, "Have faith in God!"

Mark 11:22

However, he gave the right to become God's children to everyone who believed in him.

John 1:12

My sheep respond to my voice, and I know who they are. They follow me, and I give them eternal life. They will never be lost, and no one will tear them away from me. My Father, who gave them to me, is greater than everyone else, and no one can tear them away from my Father.

John 10:27-29

Jesus said to Thomas, "You believe because you've seen me. Blessed are those who haven't seen me but believe."

John 20:29

Understand what I'm saying. The Lord will help you understand all these things.

2 Timothy 2:7

Faith assures us of things we expect and convinces us of the existence of things we cannot see.

Hebrews 11:1

No one can please God without faith. Whoever goes to God must believe that God exists and that he rewards those who seek him.

Hebrews 11:6

If any of you needs wisdom to know what you should do, you should ask God, and he will give it to you. God is generous to everyone and doesn't find fault with them. When you ask for something, don't have any doubts. A person who has doubts is like a wave that is blown by the wind and tossed by the sea. A person who has doubts shouldn't expect to receive anything from the Lord. A person who has doubts is thinking about two different things at the same time and can't make up his mind about anything.

James 1:5-8

God is faithful and reliable. If we confess our sins, he forgives them and cleanses us from everything we've done wrong.

1 John 1:9

~ EMBARRASSMENT ~

I am ashamed, my God. I am embarrassed to look at you. Our sins have piled up over our heads, and our guilt is so overwhelming that it reaches heaven.

Ezra 9:6

The LORD is near to those whose hearts are humble.
He saves those whose spirits are crushed.

Psalm 34:18

A person's pride will humiliate him,
but a humble spirit gains honor.

Proverbs 29:23

If people are ashamed of me and what I say, the Son of Man will be ashamed of those people when he comes in the glory that he shares with the Father and the holy angels.

Luke 9:26

I'm not ashamed of the Good News. It is God's power to save everyone who believes, Jews first and Greeks as well.

Romans 1:16

So never be ashamed to tell others about our Lord or be ashamed of me, his prisoner. Instead, by God's power, join me in suffering for the sake of the Good News.

2 Timothy 1:8

For this reason I suffer as I do. However, I'm not ashamed. I know whom I trust. I'm convinced that he is able to protect what he had entrusted to me until that day.

2 Timothy 1:12

Do your best to present yourself to God as a tried-and-true worker who isn't ashamed to teach the word of truth correctly.

2 Timothy 2:15

⮐ ENCOURAGEMENT ⮑

The reason I can ⌊still⌋ find hope is that I keep this one thing in mind:
the LORD's mercy.
> We were not completely wiped out.
> His compassion is never limited.
> > It is new every morning.
> > His faithfulness is great.

Lamentations 3:21-23

The LORD your God is with you.
> He is a hero who saves you.

> He happily rejoices over you,
>   renews you with his love,
>   and celebrates over you with shouts of joy.
>
> *Zephaniah 3:17b*

In the same way let your light shine in front of people. Then they will see the good that you do and praise your Father in heaven.

Matthew 5:16

I will ask the Father, and he will give you another helper who will be with you forever.

John 14:16

We can't allow ourselves to get tired of living the right way. Certainly, each of us will receive ⌊everlasting life⌋ at the proper time, if we don't give up.

Galatians 6:9

God our Father loved us and by his kindness gave us everlasting encouragement and good hope. Together with our Lord Jesus Christ, may he encourage and strengthen you to do and say everything that is good.

2 Thessalonians 2:16-17

Encourage each other every day while you have the opportunity. If you do this, none of you will be deceived by sin and become stubborn.

Hebrews 3:13

God is fair. He won't forget what you've done or the love you've shown for him.

Hebrews 6:10a

ENVY

Do not be preoccupied with evildoers.
Do not envy those who do wicked things.

Psalm 37:1

Surrender yourself to the LORD, and wait patiently for him.
   Do not be preoccupied with ⌊an evildoer⌋ who succeeds in his way
      when he carries out his schemes.

Psalm 37:7

Do not envy sinners in your heart.
   Instead, continue to fear the LORD.

Proverbs 23:17

This is what the LORD says:
   Don't let wise people brag about their wisdom.
   Don't let strong people brag about their strength.
   Don't let rich people brag about their riches.
   If they want to brag,
      they should brag that they understand and know me.
      They should brag that I, the LORD, act out of love, righteousness,

and justice on the earth.
>   This kind of bragging pleases me, declares the LORD.

Jeremiah 9:23-24

Love is patient. Love is kind. Love isn't jealous. It doesn't sing its own praises. It isn't arrogant.

1 Corinthians 13:4

We can't allow ourselves to act arrogantly and to provoke or envy each other.

Galatians 5:26

But if you are bitterly jealous and filled with self-centered ambition, don't brag. Don't say that you are wise when it isn't true.

James 3:14

Wherever there is jealousy and rivalry, there is disorder and every kind of evil.

James 3:16

❧ ETERNAL LIFE ❧

But I know that my defender lives,
>   and afterwards, he will rise on the earth.
Even after my skin has been stripped off my body,
>   I will see God in my own flesh.
I will see him with my own eyes,

not with someone else's.
My heart fails inside me!

Job 19:25-2?

God loved the world this way: He gave his only Son so that everyone
who believes in him will not die but will have eternal life.

John 3:1?

I can guarantee this truth: Those who listen to what I say and believe
in the one who sent me will have eternal life. They won't be judged
because they have already passed from death to life.

John 5:2?

My Father wants all those who see the Son and believe in him to have
eternal life. He wants me to bring them back to life on the last day.

John 6:4?

My sheep respond to my voice, and I know who they are. They follow
me, and I give them eternal life. They will never be lost, and no one will
tear them away from me.

John 10:27-2?

Jesus said to her, "I am the one who brings people back to life, and I
am life itself. Those who believe in me will live even if they die.
Everyone who lives and believes in me will never die. Do you believe
that?"

John 11:25-2?

The reward for sin is death, but the gift that God freely gives is everlasting life found in Christ Jesus our Lord.

Romans 6:23

I'm telling you a mystery. Not all of us will die, but we will all be changed. It will happen in an instant, in a split second at the sound of the last trumpet. Indeed, that trumpet will sound, and then the dead will come back to life. They will be changed so that they can live forever.

1 Corinthians 15:51-52

This is the testimony: God has given us eternal life, and this life is found in his Son.

1 John 5:11

I've written this to those who believe in the Son of God so that they will know that they have eternal life.

1 John 5:13

We know that the Son of God has come and has given us understanding so that we know the real God. We are in the one who is real, his Son Jesus Christ. This Jesus Christ is the real God and eternal life.

1 John 5:20

❧ EXPECTANCY ❧

Wait with hope for the LORD.
Be strong, and let your heart be courageous.
Yes, wait with hope for the LORD.

Psalm 27:1

Wait calmly for God alone, my soul,
    because my hope comes from him.

Psalm 62.

I wait for the LORD, my soul waits,
    and with hope I wait for his word.

Psalm 130:

On that day ⌊his people⌋ will say,
    " This is our God; we have waited for him, and now he will save us
    This is the LORD; we have waited for him.
        Let us rejoice and be glad because he will save us."

Isaiah 25:

I consider our present sufferings insignificant compared to the glory
that will soon be revealed to us. All creation is eagerly waiting for God
to reveal who his children are.

Romans 8:18-1

FAILURE **77**

It's not that I've already reached the goal or have already completed the course. But I run to win that which Jesus Christ has already won for me.

Philippians 3:12

We must continue to hold firmly to our declaration of faith. The one who made the promise is faithful.

Hebrews 10:23

The Lord isn't slow to do what he promised, as some people think. Rather, he is patient for your sake. He doesn't want to destroy anyone but wants all people to have an opportunity to turn to him and change the way they think and act.

2 Peter 3:9

I'm coming soon! I will bring my reward with me to pay all people based on what they have done. I am the A and the Z, the first and the last, the beginning and the end.

Revelation 22:12-13

❧ FAILURE ❧

David also told his son Solomon, "Be strong and courageous, and do the work. Don't be afraid or terrified. The LORD God, my God, will be with you. He will not abandon you before all the work on the LORD's temple is finished."

1 Chronicles 28:20

A person's steps are directed by the LORD,
  and the LORD delights in his way.
When he falls, he will not be thrown down headfirst
  because the LORD holds on to his hand.

Psalm 37:23-24

As far as the east is from the west—
  that is how far he has removed our rebellious acts from himself.

Psalm 103:12

So those who are believers in Christ Jesus can no longer be
condemned.

Romans 8:1

We know that all things work together for the good of those who love
God—those whom he has called according to his plan.

Romans 8:28

Who are you to criticize someone else's servant? The Lord will
determine whether his servant has been successful. The servant will
be successful because the Lord makes him successful.

Romans 14:4

So, then, brothers and sisters, don't let anyone move you off the
foundation ⌊of your faith⌋. Always excel in the work you do for the Lord.
You know that the hard work you do for the Lord is not pointless.

1 Corinthians 15:58

Put up with each other, and forgive each other if anyone has a complaint.
Forgive as the Lord forgave you.

Colossians 3:13

God is faithful and reliable. If we confess our sins, he forgives them and
cleanses us from everything we've done wrong.

1 John 1:9

∾ **FAITH** ∾

He told them, "Because you have so little faith. I can guarantee this truth: If
your faith is the size of a mustard seed, you can say to this mountain,
'Move from here to there,' and it will move. Nothing will be impossible
for you."

Matthew 17:20b

That's why I tell you to have faith that you have already received whatever
you pray for, and it will be yours.

Mark 11:24

Now that we have God's approval by faith, we have peace with God
because of what our Lord Jesus Christ has done.

Romans 5:1

God saved you through faith as an act of kindness. You had nothing to do
with it. Being saved is a gift from God.

Ephesians 2:8

Faith assures us of things we expect and convinces us of the existence
of things we cannot see.

Hebrews 11:1

No one can please God without faith. Whoever goes to God must
believe that God exists and that he rewards those who seek him.

Hebrews 11:6

When you ask for something, don't have any doubts. A person who has
doubts is like a wave that is blown by the wind and tossed by the sea.

James 1:6

(Prayers offered in faith will save those who are sick, and the Lord will
cure them.) If you have sinned, you will be forgiven.

James 5:15

Although you have never seen Christ, you love him. You don't see him
now, but you believe in him. You are extremely happy with joy and
praise that can hardly be expressed in words as you obtain the
salvation that is the goal of your faith.

1 Peter 1:8-9

✎ FAITHFULNESS ✎ OF GOD

The word of the LORD is correct,
and everything he does is trustworthy.

Psalm 33:4

But you, O Lord, are a compassionate and merciful God.
You are patient, always faithful and ready to forgive.

Psalm 86:15

He will cover you with his feathers,
and under his wings you will find refuge.
His truth is your shield and armor.

Psalm 91:4

The LORD is good.
His mercy endures forever.
His faithfulness endures throughout every generation.

Psalm 100:5

His mercy toward us is powerful.
The LORD's faithfulness endures forever.

Psalm 117:2

We were not completely wiped out.
His compassion is never limited.
   It is new every morning.
   His faithfulness is great.

Lamentations 3:22-23

What if some of them were unfaithful? Can their unfaithfulness cancel God's faithfulness? That would be unthinkable! God is honest, and everyone else is a liar.

Romans 3:3-4a

✺ FAMILY ✺

Then the LORD God said, "It is not good for the man to be alone. I will make a helper who is right for him."

Genesis 2:18

Take to heart these words that I give you today. Repeat them to your children. Talk about them when you're at home or away, when you lie down or get up.

Deuteronomy 6:6-7

But if you don't want to serve the LORD, then choose today whom you will serve. . . . My family and I will still serve the LORD.

Joshua 24:15

Train a child in the way he should go,
   and even when he is old he will not turn away from it.

Proverbs 22:6

A righteous person's father will certainly rejoice.
Someone who has a wise son will enjoy him.

Proverbs 23:24

Who can find a wife with a strong character?
She is worth far more than jewels. . . .
Her children and her husband
   stand up and bless her.
In addition, he sings her praises.

Proverbs 31:10, 28

Children, obey your parents because you are Christians. This is the right thing to do. . . .
   Fathers, don't make your children bitter about life. Instead, bring them up in Christian discipline and instruction.

Ephesians 6:1,4

❧ FATHERHOOD OF GOD ❧

The God who is in his holy dwelling place
  is the father of the fatherless and the defender of widows.

Psalm 68:5

Do not reject the discipline of the LORD, my son,
  and do not resent his warning,
    because the LORD warns the one he loves,
      even as a father warns a son with whom he is pleased.

Proverbs 3:11-12

Even though you're evil, you know how to give good gifts to your
children. So how much more will your Father in heaven give good
things to those who ask him?

Matthew 7:11

However, he gave the right to become God's children to everyone who
believed in him.

John 1:12

Certainly, all who are guided by God's Spirit are God's children.

Romans 8:14

You are all God's children by believing in Christ Jesus.

Galatians 3:26

Because you are God's children, God has sent the Spirit of his Son into us to call out, "Abba! Father!" So you are no longer slaves but God's children. Since you are God's children, God has also made you heirs.

Galatians 4:6-7

There is one Lord . . . one God and Father of all, who is over everything, through everything, and in everything.

Ephesians 4:5-6

Consider this: The Father has given us his love. He loves us so much that we are actually called God's dear children. And that's what we are. For this reason the world doesn't recognize us, and it didn't recognize him either.

1 John 3:1

∾ FEAR ∽

The LORD is my light and my salvation.
    Who is there to fear?
The LORD is my life's fortress.
    Who is there to be afraid of?

Psalm 27:1

I trust God.
I am not afraid.
    What can mortals do to me?

Psalm 56:11

He will put his angels in charge of you
   to protect you in all your ways.

Psalm 91:11

Don't be afraid, because I am with you.
Don't be intimidated; I am your God.
   I will strengthen you.
   I will help you.
   I will support you with my victorious right hand.

Isaiah 41:10

My friends, I can guarantee that you don't need to be afraid of those
who kill the body. After that they can't do anything more. I'll show you
the one you should be afraid of. Be afraid of the one who has the
power to throw you into hell after killing you. I'm warning you to be
afraid of him.

Luke 12:4-5

I'm leaving you peace. I'm giving you my peace. I don't give you the
kind of peace that the world gives. So don't be troubled or cowardly.

John 14:27

You haven't received the spirit of slaves that leads you into fear again.
Instead, you have received the spirit of God's adopted children by
which we call out, "Abba! Father!"

Romans 8:15

God didn't give us a cowardly spirit but a spirit of power, love, and good judgment.

2 Timothy 1:7

No fear exists where his love is. Rather, perfect love gets rid of fear, because fear involves punishment. The person who lives in fear doesn't have perfect love.

1 John 4:18

◦◦ FORGIVENESS ◦◦

    I admit that I am rebellious.
    My sin is always in front of me.
I have sinned against you, especially you.
I have done what you consider evil.
    So you hand down justice when you speak,
        and you are blameless when you judge.

Psalm 51:3-4

Purify me from sin with hyssop, and I will be clean.
Wash me, and I will be whiter than snow.
    Let me hear ⌊sounds of⌋ joy and gladness.
    Let the bones that you have broken dance.
Hide your face from my sins,
    and wipe out all that I have done wrong.

Psalm 51:7-9

As high as the heavens are above the earth—
    that is how vast his mercy is toward those who fear him.
As far as the east is from the west—
    that is how far he has removed our rebellious acts from himself.

Psalm 103:11-12

I alone am the one who is going to wipe away your rebellious actions
    for my own sake.
        I will not remember your sins ⌊anymore⌋.

Isaiah 43:25

If you forgive the failures of others, your heavenly Father will also
forgive you. But if you don't forgive others, your Father will not forgive
your failures.

Matthew 6:14-15

So those who are believers in Christ Jesus can no longer be
condemned.

Romans 8:1

God has rescued us from the power of darkness and has brought us
into the kingdom of his Son, whom he loves. His Son paid the price to
free us, which means that our sins are forgiven.

Colossians 1:13-14

Put up with each other, and forgive each other if anyone has a
complaint. Forgive as the Lord forgave you.

Colossians 3:13

God is faithful and reliable. If we confess our sins, he forgives them
and cleanses us from everything we've done wrong.

1 John 1:9

❧ FREEDOM ❧

The Spirit of the Lord is with me.
> He has anointed me
>> to tell the Good News to the poor.
> He has sent me
>> to announce forgiveness to the prisoners of sin
>>> and the restoring of sight to the blind,
>> to forgive those who have been shattered by sin.

Luke 4:18

You will know the truth, and the truth will set you free.

John 8:32

So if the Son sets you free, you will be absolutely free.

John 8:36

Certainly, sin shouldn't have power over you because you're not
controlled by laws, but by God's favor.

Romans 6:14

Now you have been freed from sin and have become God's slaves. This results in a holy life and, finally, in everlasting life.

Romans 6:2.

So those who are believers in Christ Jesus can no longer be condemned. The standards of the Spirit, who gives life through Christ Jesus, have set you free from the standards of sin and death.

Romans 8:1-.

Christ has freed us so that we may enjoy the benefits of freedom. Therefore, be firm ⌊in this freedom⌋, and don't become slaves again.

Galatians 5:

You were indeed called to be free, brothers and sisters. Don't turn this freedom into an excuse for your corrupt nature to express itself. Rather, serve each other through love.

Galatians 5:1

FRIENDSHIP

Whoever forgives an offense seeks love,
but whoever keeps bringing up the issue
separates the closest of friends.

Proverbs 17:

A friend always loves,
  and a brother is born to share trouble.

Proverbs 17:17

Friends can destroy one another,
  but a loving friend can stick closer than family.

Proverbs 18:24

Wounds made by a friend are intended to help,
  but an enemy's kisses are too much to bear.

Proverbs 27:6

The greatest love you can show is to give your life for your friends.
You are my friends if you obey my commandments.

John 15:13-14

Brothers and sisters, I encourage all of you in the name of our Lord
Jesus Christ to agree with each other and not to split into opposing
groups. I want you to be united in your understanding and opinions.

1 Corinthians 1:10

❧ FRUSTRATION ❧

A fool expresses all his emotions,
  but a wise person controls them.

Proverbs 29:11

I'm leaving you peace. I'm giving you my peace. I don't give you the kind of peace that the world gives. So don't be troubled or cowardly.

John 14:2

But that's not all. We also brag when we are suffering. We know that suffering creates endurance, endurance creates character, and character creates confidence. We're not ashamed to have this confidence, because God's love has been poured into our hearts by the Holy Spirit, who has been given to us.

Romans 5:3-5

[Love] isn't rude. It doesn't think about itself. It isn't irritable. It doesn't keep track of wrongs.

1 Corinthians 13:5

Be angry without sinning. Don't go to bed angry.

Ephesians 4:26

Get rid of your bitterness, hot tempers, anger, loud quarreling, cursing, and hatred. Be kind to each other, sympathetic, forgiving each other as God has forgiven you through Christ.

Ephesians 4:31-32

Don't be concerned only about your own interests, but also be concerned about the interests of others.

Philippians 2:4

Never worry about anything. But in every situation let God know what you need in prayers and requests while giving thanks. Then God's peace, which goes beyond anything we can imagine, will guard your thoughts and emotions through Christ Jesus.

Finally, brothers and sisters, keep your thoughts on whatever is right or deserves praise: things that are true, honorable, fair, pure, acceptable, or commendable.

Philippians 4:6-8

Also, let Christ's peace control you. God has called you into this peace by bringing you into one body. Be thankful.

Colossians 3:15

Remember this, my dear brothers and sisters: Everyone should be quick to listen, slow to speak, and should not get angry easily. An angry person doesn't do what God approves of.

James 1:19-20

∾ **FUTURE** ∾

If only they would fear me and obey all my commandments as long as they live! Then things would go well for them and their children forever.

Deuteronomy 5:29

I know the plans that I have for you, declares the LORD. They are plans
for peace and not disaster, plans to give you a future filled with hope.

Jeremiah 29:11

So don't ever worry about tomorrow. After all, tomorrow will worry
about itself. Each day has enough trouble of its own.

Matthew 6:34

Therefore, be alert, because you don't know on what day your Lord
will return.

Matthew 24:42

But as Scripture says:
  "No eye has seen,
     no ear has heard,
        and no mind has imagined
           the things that God has prepared
              for those who love him."

1 Corinthians 2:9

I'm telling you a mystery. Not all of us will die, but we will all be
changed. It will happen in an instant, in a split second at the sound of
the last trumpet. Indeed, that trumpet will sound, and then the dead
will come back to life. They will be changed so that they can live
forever.

1 Corinthians 15:51-52

Pay attention to this! You're saying, "Today or tomorrow we will go into some city, stay there a year, conduct business, and make money." You don't know what will happen tomorrow. What is life? You are a mist that is seen for a moment and then disappears. Instead, you should say, "If the Lord wants us to, we will live and carry out our plans."

James 4:13-15

❧ GOD'S WILL ❧

Make your ways known to me, O LORD,
    and teach me your paths.
Lead me in your truth and teach me
    because you are God, my savior.
        I wait all day long for you.

Psalm 25:4-5

⌊The LORD says,⌋
    "I will instruct you.
    I will teach you the way that you should go.
    I will advise you as my eyes watch over you."

Psalm 32:8

A person's steps are directed by the LORD,
    and the LORD delights in his way.

Psalm 37:23

Trust the LORD with all your heart,
    and do not rely on your own understanding.
In all your ways acknowledge him,
    and he will make your paths smooth.

Proverbs 3:5-6

Entrust your efforts to the LORD,
    and your plans will succeed.

Proverbs 16:3

You mortals, the LORD has told you what is good.
    This is what the LORD requires from you:
        to do what is right,
            to love mercy,
                and to live humbly with your God.

Micah 6:8

When the Spirit of Truth comes, he will guide you into the full truth. He won't speak on his own. He will speak what he hears and will tell you about things to come.

John 16:13

It is God who produces in you the desires and actions that please him.
Philippians 2:13

Whatever happens, give thanks, because it is God's will in Christ Jesus that you do this.

1 Thessalonians 5:18

∾ GOOD NEWS ∾

How beautiful on the mountains are the feet of the messenger
who announces the good news, "All is well."
He brings the good news,
announces salvation,
and tells Zion that its God rules as king.

Isaiah 52:7

He said, "The time has come, and the kingdom of God is near. Change the
way you think and act, and believe the Good News."

Mark 1:15

Then Jesus said to them, "So wherever you go in the world, tell everyone
the Good News."

Mark 16:15

The Spirit of the Lord is with me.
He has anointed me
to tell the Good News to the poor.
He has sent me
to announce forgiveness to the prisoners of sin
and the restoring of sight to the blind,
to forgive those who have been shattered by sin.

Luke 4:18

He said to them, "Scripture says that the Messiah would suffer and that he would come back to life on the third day. Scripture also says that by the authority of Jesus people would be told to turn to God and change the way they think and act so that their sins will be forgiven. This would be told to people from all nations, beginning in the city of Jerusalem."

Luke 24:46-47

God loved the world this way: He gave his only Son so that everyone who believes in him will not die but will have eternal life.

John 3:16

We're spreading the Good News to you to turn you away from these worthless gods to the living God. The living God made the sky, the land, the sea, and everything in them.

Acts 14:15b

I'm not ashamed of the Good News. It is God's power to save everyone who believes, Jews first and Greeks as well.

Romans 1:16

❧ GOODNESS OF GOD ❧

The LORD is good and decent.
    That is why he teaches sinners the way they should live.

Psalm 25:8

Taste and see that the LORD is good.
   Blessed is the person who takes refuge in him.

Psalm 34:8

God is truly good to Israel,
   to those whose lives are pure.

Psalm 73:1

You, O Lord, are good and forgiving,
   full of mercy toward everyone who calls out to you.

Psalm 86:5

You are good, and you do good things.
   Teach me your laws.

Psalm 119:68a

Give thanks to the LORD because he is good,
   because his mercy endures forever.

Psalm 136:1

The LORD is good to everyone
   and has compassion for everything that he has made.

Psalm 145:9

The LORD is good.
   ⌊He is⌋ a fortress in the day of trouble.
   He knows those who seek shelter in him.

Nahum 1:7

❧ GOSSIP ❧

⌊The LORD continued,⌋ "Never spread false rumors. Don't join forces with wicked people by giving false testimony."

Exodus 23:1a

Whoever gossips gives away secrets,
  but whoever is trustworthy in spirit can keep a secret.

Proverbs 11:13

A devious person spreads quarrels.
A gossip separates the closest of friends.

Proverbs 16:28

The words of a gossip are swallowed greedily,
  and they go down into a person's innermost being.

Proverbs 18:8

Whoever goes around as a gossip tells secrets.
  Do not associate with a person whose mouth is always open.

Proverbs 20:19

Without wood a fire goes out,
  and without gossip a quarrel dies down.

Proverbs 26:20

❧ GRIEF ❧

Blessed are those who mourn.
They will be comforted.

Matthew 5:4

Come to me, all who are tired from carrying heavy loads, and I will give you rest.

Matthew 11:28

Jesus said to her, "I am the one who brings people back to life, and I am life itself. Those who believe in me will live even if they die. Everyone who lives and believes in me will never die. Do you believe that?"

John 11:25-26

I'm leaving you peace. I'm giving you my peace. I don't give you the kind of peace that the world gives. So don't be troubled or cowardly.

John 14:27

At the same time the Spirit also helps us in our weakness, because we don't know how to pray for what we need. But the Spirit intercedes along with our groans that cannot be expressed in words.

Romans 8:26

We know that all things work together for the good of those who love God—those whom he has called according to his plan.

Romans 8:2

Praise the God and Father of our Lord Jesus Christ! He is the Father who is compassionate and the God who gives comfort. He comforts us whenever we suffer. That is why whenever other people suffer, we are able to comfort them by using the same comfort we have received from God.

2 Corinthians 1:3

Dear friends, don't be surprised by the fiery troubles that are coming in order to test you. Don't feel as though something strange is happening to you, but be happy as you share Christ's sufferings. Then you will also be full of joy when he appears again in his glory.

1 Peter 4:12-

God, who shows you his kindness and who has called you through Christ Jesus to his eternal glory, will restore you, strengthen you, make you strong, and support you as you suffer for a little while.

1 Peter 5:

He will wipe every tear from their eyes. There won't be any more death. There won't be any grief, crying, or pain, because the first things have disappeared.

Revelation 2:

~ GROWTH ~

Brothers and sisters, in view of all we have just shared about God's compassion toward us, I encourage you to offer your bodies as living sacrifices, dedicated to God and pleasing to him. This kind of worship is appropriate for you. Don't become like the people of this world. Instead, change the way you think. Then you will always be able to determine what God really wants—what is good, pleasing, and perfect.

Romans 12:1-2

As all of us reflect the Lord's glory with faces that are not covered with veils, we are being changed into his image with ever-increasing glory. This comes from the Lord, who is the Spirit.

2 Corinthians 3:18

Instead, as we lovingly speak the truth, we will grow up completely in our relationship to Christ, who is the head. He makes the whole body fit together and unites it through the support of every joint. As each and every part does its job, he makes the body grow so that it builds itself up in love.

Ephesians 4:15-16

I'm convinced that God, who began this good work in you, will carry it through to completion on the day of Christ Jesus.

Philippians 1:6

We ask this so that you will live the kind of lives that prove you belong
to the Lord. Then you will want to please him in every way as you grow
in producing every kind of good work by this knowledge about God.

Colossians 1:1

Practice these things. Devote your life to them so that everyone can
see your progress.

1 Timothy 4:1

Stay away from lusts which tempt young people. Pursue what has
God's approval. Pursue faith, love, and peace together with those who
worship the Lord with a pure heart.

2 Timothy 2:2

Desire God's pure word as newborn babies desire milk. Then you will
grow in your salvation.

1 Peter 2:

Because of this, make every effort to add integrity to your faith; and to
integrity add knowledge; to knowledge add self-control; to self-control
add endurance; to endurance add godliness.

2 Peter 1:5

But grow in the good will and knowledge of our Lord and Savior Jesus
Christ. Glory belongs to him now and for that eternal day! Amen.

2 Peter 3:1

∽ GUIDANCE ∽

Make your ways known to me, O LORD,
  and teach me your paths.
Lead me in your truth and teach me
  because you are God, my savior.
    I wait all day long for you.

Psalm 25:4-5

⌊The LORD says,⌋
  "I will instruct you.
  I will teach you the way that you should go.
  I will advise you as my eyes watch over you."

Psalm 32:8

Your word is a lamp for my feet
  and a light for my path.

Psalm 119:105

Trust the LORD with all your heart,
  and do not rely on your own understanding.
In all your ways acknowledge him,
  and he will make your paths smooth.

Proverbs 3:5-6

A nation will fall when there is no direction,
but with many advisers there is victory.

Proverbs 11:1

Entrust your efforts to the LORD,
and your plans will succeed.

Proverbs 16:

A person may plan his own journey,
but the LORD directs his steps.

Proverbs 16:

You will hear a voice behind you saying, "This is the way. Follow it, whether it turns to the right or to the left."

Isaiah 30:2

When the Spirit of Truth comes, he will guide you into the full truth. He won't speak on his own. He will speak what he hears and will tell you about things to come.

John 16:

It is God who produces in you the desires and actions that please him.

Philippians 2:

Every Scripture passage is inspired by God. All of them are useful for teaching, pointing out errors, correcting people, and training them for a life that has God's approval.

2 Timothy 3:

f any of you needs wisdom to know what you should do, you should
ask God, and he will give it to you. God is generous to everyone and
doesn't find fault with them.

James 1:5

❧ GUILT ❧

I made my sins known to you, and I did not cover up my guilt.
I decided to confess them to you, O LORD.
   Then you forgave all my sins.

Psalm 32:5

Wash me thoroughly from my guilt,
   and cleanse me from my sin. . . .
Purify me from sin with hyssop, and I will be clean.
Wash me, and I will be whiter than snow.

Psalm 51:2,7

   The sacrifice pleasing to God is a broken spirit.
   O God, you do not despise a broken and sorrowful heart.

Psalm 51:17

As high as the heavens are above the earth—
   that is how vast his mercy is toward those who fear him.
As far as the east is from the west—
   that is how far he has removed our rebellious acts from himself.

Psalm 103:11-12

Whoever covers over his sins does not prosper.
Whoever confesses and abandons them receives compassion.

Proverbs 28:1

He was wounded for our rebellious acts.
He was crushed for our sins.
    He was punished so that we could have peace,
        and we received healing from his wounds.
We have all strayed like sheep.
    Each one of us has turned to go his own way,
        . and the LORD has laid all our sins on him.

Isaiah 53:5-

So if the Son sets you free, you will be absolutely free.

John 8:3

Because all people have sinned, they have fallen short of God's glory.
They receive God's approval freely by an act of his kindness through
the price Christ Jesus paid to set us free ⌊from sin⌋.

Romans 3:23-2

So those who are believers in Christ Jesus can no longer be
condemned.

Romans 8.

God is faithful and reliable. If we confess our sins, he forgives them
and cleanses us from everything we've done wrong.

1 John 1.

⌘ HAPPINESS ⌘

Blessed is the person whose disobedience is forgiven
   and whose sin is pardoned.

Psalm 32:1

Taste and see that the LORD is good.
   Blessed is the person who takes refuge in him.

Psalm 34:8

Blessed is the one who has concern for helpless people.
   The LORD will rescue him in times of trouble.

Psalm 41:1

Why are you discouraged, my soul?
   Why are you so restless?
     Put your hope in God,
       because I will still praise him.
         He is my savior and my God.

Psalm 42:11

This is the day the LORD has made.
   Let's rejoice and be glad today!

Psalm 118:24

Blessed are those who obey his written instructions.
    They wholeheartedly search for him.

Psalm 119:

A joyful heart is good medicine,
    but depression drains one's strength.

Proverbs 17:2

❧ HATRED ❧

Never get revenge. Never hold a grudge against any of your people.
Instead, love your neighbor as you love yourself. I am the LORD.

Leviticus 19:

Hate starts quarrels,
    but love covers every wrong.

Proverbs 10:

Whoever conceals hatred has lying lips.
Whoever spreads slander is a fool.

Proverbs 10:

Bless those who persecute you. Bless them, and don't curse them. . . .
Don't pay people back with evil for the evil they do to you. Focus your
thoughts on those things that are considered noble. As much as it is
possible, live in peace with everyone. Don't take revenge, dear friends.

nstead, let God's anger take care of it. After all, Scripture says, "I alone
ave the right to take revenge. I will pay back, says the Lord."

Romans 12:14, 17-19

`ry to live peacefully with everyone, and try to live holy lives, because
 you don't, you will not see the Lord. Make sure that everyone has
indness from God so that bitterness doesn't take root and grow up to
ause trouble that corrupts many of you.

Hebrews 12:14-15

HEALING

Praise the LORD, my soul,
  and never forget all the good he has done:
He is the one who forgives all your sins,
  the one who heals all your diseases.

Psalm 103:2-3

A joyful heart is good medicine,
  but depression drains one's strength.

Proverbs 17:22

He was wounded for our rebellious acts.
  He was crushed for our sins.
    He was punished so that we could have peace,
      and we received healing from his wounds.

Isaiah 53:5

Heal me, O LORD, and I will be healed.
  Rescue me, and I will be rescued.
    You are the one I praise.

Jeremiah 17:14

That is why we are not discouraged. Though outwardly we are wearing out, inwardly we are renewed day by day.

2 Corinthians 4:16

But he told me: "My kindness is all you need. My power is strongest when you are weak." So I will brag even more about my weaknesses in order that Christ's power will live in me. Therefore, I accept weakness, mistreatment, hardship, persecution, and difficulties suffered for Christ. It's clear that when I'm weak, I'm strong.

2 Corinthians 12:9-10

If you are sick, call for the church leaders. Have them pray for you and anoint you with olive oil in the name of the Lord. (Prayers offered in faith will save those who are sick, and the Lord will cure them.) If you have sinned, you will be forgiven. So admit your sins to each other, and pray for each other so that you will be healed.
  Prayers offered by those who have God's approval are effective.

James 5:14-16

~ HEAVEN ~

Not everyone who says to me, "Lord, Lord!" will enter the kingdom of heaven, but only the person who does what my Father in heaven wants.

Matthew 7:21

My Father's house has many rooms. If that were not true, would I have told you that I'm going to prepare a place for you?

John 14:2

We, however, are citizens of heaven. We look forward to the Lord Jesus Christ coming from heaven as our Savior.

Philippians 3:20

Christ didn't go into a holy place made by human hands. He didn't go into a model of the real thing. Instead, he went into heaven to appear in God's presence on our behalf.

Hebrews 9:24

I heard every creature in heaven, on earth, under the earth, and on the sea. Every creature in those places was singing,
   "To the one who sits on the throne and to the lamb
      be praise, honor, glory, and power forever and ever."

Revelation 5:13

He will wipe every tear from their eyes. There won't be any more death. There won't be any grief, crying, or pain, because the first things have disappeared.

Revelation 21:4

Nothing unclean, no one who does anything detestable, and no liars will ever enter it. Only those whose names are written in the lamb's Book of Life will enter it.

Revelation 21:27

❧ HELP OF GOD ❧

The LORD is my rock and my fortress and my Savior,
   my God, my rock in whom I take refuge,
      my shield, and the strength of my salvation,
         my stronghold.

Psalm 18:2

You are my hiding place.
You protect me from trouble.
You surround me with joyous songs of salvation.

Psalm 32:7

We wait for the LORD.
   He is our help and our shield.

Psalm 33:20

God is our refuge and strength,
   an ever-present help in times of trouble.

Psalm 46:1

God is my helper!
The Lord is the provider for my life.

Psalm 54:4

I look up toward the mountains.
   Where can I find help?
My help comes from the LORD,
   the maker of heaven and earth.

Psalm 121:1-2

The LORD is good.
   ⌊He is⌋ a fortress in the day of trouble.
   He knows those who seek shelter in him.

Nahum 1:7

I will ask the Father, and he will give you another helper who will be
with you forever.

John 14:16

However, the helper, the Holy Spirit, whom the Father will send in my
name, will teach you everything. He will remind you of everything that
I have ever told you.

John 14:26

At the same time the Spirit also helps us in our weakness, because we don't know how to pray for what we need. But the Spirit intercedes along with our groans that cannot be expressed in words.

Romans 8:26

My dear children, I'm writing this to you so that you will not sin. Yet, if anyone does sin, we have Jesus Christ, who has God's full approval. He speaks on our behalf when we come into the presence of the Father.

1 John 2:1

‮❧‬ HELPLESSNESS ‮❧‬

You have seen ⌊it⌋; yes, you have taken note of trouble and grief
and placed them under your control.
    The victim entrusts himself to you.
You alone have been the helper of orphans.

Psalm 10:14

Hear, O LORD, and have pity on me!
O LORD, be my helper!

Psalm 30:10

Blessed is the one who has concern for helpless people.
    The LORD will rescue him in times of trouble.

Psalm 41:1

Whoever gives to the poor lacks nothing.
Whoever ignores the poor receives many curses.

Proverbs 28:27

Look at it this way: At the right time, while we were still helpless,
Christ died for ungodly people.

Romans 5:6

At the same time the Spirit also helps us in our weakness, because we
don't know how to pray for what we need. But the Spirit intercedes
along with our groans that cannot be expressed in words.

Romans 8:26

Pure, unstained religion, according to God our Father, is to take care
of orphans and widows when they suffer and to remain uncorrupted by
this world.

James 1:27

❧ **HOPE** ❧

Why are you discouraged, my soul?
   Why are you so restless?
      Put your hope in God,
         because I will still praise him.
            He is my savior and my God.

Psalm 42:11

You are my hope, O Almighty LORD.
You have been my confidence ever since I was young.

Psalm 71:5

But that's not all. We also brag when we are suffering. We know that suffering creates endurance, endurance creates character, and character creates confidence. We're not ashamed to have this confidence, because God's love has been poured into our hearts by the Holy Spirit, who has been given to us.

Romans 5:3-5

We were saved with this hope in mind. If we hope for something we already see, it's not really hope. Who hopes for what can be seen? But if we hope for what we don't see, we eagerly wait for it with perseverance.

Romans 8:24-25

May God, the source of hope, fill you with joy and peace through your faith in him. Then you will overflow with hope by the power of the Holy Spirit.

Romans 15:13

Love never stops being patient, never stops believing, never stops hoping, never gives up.

1 Corinthians 13:7

God wanted his people throughout the world to know the glorious riches of this mystery—which is Christ living in you, giving you the hope of glory.

Colossians 1:27

God our Father loved us and by his kindness gave us everlasting encouragement and good hope. Together with our Lord Jesus Christ, may he encourage and strengthen you to do and say everything that is good.

2 Thessalonians 2:16-17

As a result, God in his kindness has given us his approval and we have become heirs who have the confidence that we have everlasting life.

Titus 3:7

Faith assures us of things we expect and convinces us of the existence of things we cannot see.

Hebrews 11:1

❧ HUMILITY ❧

However, if my people, who are called by my name,
    will humble themselves,
    pray, search for me, and turn from their evil ways,
then I will hear ⌊their prayer⌋ from heaven, forgive their sins,
    and heal their country.

2 Chronicles 7:14

You save humble people,
  but you bring down a conceited look.

Psalm 18:27

As a father has compassion for his children,
  so the LORD has compassion for those who fear him.
He certainly knows what we are made of.
  He bears in mind that we are dust.

Psalm 103:13-14

Arrogance comes,
  then comes shame,
    but wisdom remains with humble people.

Proverbs 11:2

I have made all these things.
  "That is why all these things have come into being,"
    declares the LORD.
I will pay attention to those
  who are humble and sorry ⌊for their sins⌋
    and who tremble at my word.

Isaiah 66:2

Everyone who honors himself will be humbled, but the person who
humbles himself will be honored.

Luke 18:14b

Because of the kindness that God has shown me, I ask you not to think of yourselves more highly than you should. Instead, your thoughts should lead you to use good judgment based on what God has given each of you as believers.

Romans 12:3

Don't act out of selfish ambition or be conceited. Instead, humbly think of others as being better than yourselves. Don't be concerned only about your own interests, but also be concerned about the interests of others. Have the same attitude that Christ Jesus had.
> Although he was in the form of God and equal with God,
>> he did not take advantage of this equality.
> Instead, he emptied himself by taking on the form of a servant,
>> by becoming like other humans,
>> by having a human appearance.
> He humbled himself by becoming obedient to the point of death,
>> death on a cross.

Philippians 2:3-8

Humble yourselves in the Lord's presence. Then he will give you a high position.

James 4:10

Furthermore, all of you must serve each other with humility, because
God opposes the arrogant but favors the humble. Be humbled by
God's power so that when the right time comes he will honor you.

1 Peter 5:5b-6

HURTS

The LORD is near to those whose hearts are humble.
He saves those whose spirits are crushed.

Psalm 34:18

He is the healer of the brokenhearted.
He is the one who bandages their wounds.

Psalm 147:3

Blessed are you when people insult you,
   persecute you,
      lie, and say all kinds of evil things about you because of me.
Rejoice and be glad because you have a great reward in heaven!
   The prophets who lived before you were persecuted in these ways.

Matthew 5:11-12

Come to me, all who are tired from carrying heavy loads, and I will
give you rest.

Matthew 11:28

Don't take revenge, dear friends. Instead, let God's anger take care of it. After all, Scripture says, "I alone have the right to take revenge. I will pay back, says the Lord."

Romans 12:19

Be kind to each other, sympathetic, forgiving each other as God has forgiven you through Christ.

Ephesians 4:32

⚘ IMMATURITY ⚘

When I was a child, I spoke like a child, thought like a child, and reasoned like a child. When I became an adult, I no longer used childish ways.

1 Corinthians 13:11

We spread the message about Christ as we instruct and teach everyone with all the wisdom there is. We want to present everyone as mature Christian people.

Colossians 1:28

Don't let anyone look down on you for being young. Instead, make your speech, behavior, love, faith, and purity an example for other believers.

1 Timothy 4:12

Stay away from lusts which tempt young people. Pursue what has
God's approval. Pursue faith, love, and peace together with those who
worship the Lord with a pure heart.

2 Timothy 2:22

You have forgotten the encouraging words that God speaks to you as
his children:
"My child, pay attention when the Lord disciplines you.
   Don't give up when he corrects you.
The Lord disciplines everyone he loves.
   He severely disciplines everyone he accepts as his child."

Hebrews 12:5-6

Endure until your testing is over. Then you will be mature and
complete, and you won't need anything.

James 1:4

✎ INDECISIVENESS ✎

But if you don't want to serve the LORD, then choose today whom you
will serve. . . . My family and I will still serve the LORD.

Joshua 24:15

In addition, the Glory of Israel does not lie or change his mind,
because he is not a mortal who changes his mind.

1 Samuel 15:29

Elijah stood up in front of all the people and asked them, "How long will you try to have it both ways? If the LORD is God, follow him; if Baal is God, follow him." The people didn't say a word.

1 Kings 18:21

A person's steps are directed by the LORD,
  and the LORD delights in his way.
When he falls, he will not be thrown down headfirst
  because the LORD holds on to his hand.

Psalm 37:23-24

How can a young person keep his life pure?
  ⌊He can do it⌋ by holding on to your word.

Psalm 119:9

If I climb upward on the rays of the morning sun
  ⌊or⌋ land on the most distant shore of the sea where the sun sets,
    even there your hand would guide me
      and your right hand would hold on to me.

Psalm 139:9-10

When you walk around, they will lead you.
  When you lie down, they will watch over you.
  When you wake up, they will talk to you
    because the command is a lamp,

the teachings are a light,
    and the warnings from discipline are the path of life

Proverbs 6:22-2

You will hear a voice behind you saying, "This is the way. Follow it,
whether it turns to the right or to the left."

Isaiah 30:2

What should I do with you, Ephraim?
What should I do with you, Judah?
    Your love is like fog in the morning.
        It disappears as quickly as the morning dew.

Hosea 6

If any of you needs wisdom to know what you should do, you should
ask God, and he will give it to you. God is generous to everyone and
doesn't find fault with them. When you ask for something, don't have
any doubts. A person who has doubts is like a wave that is blown by
the wind and tossed by the sea.

James 1:5-

❧ INDIFFERENCE ❧

Gullible people kill themselves because of their turning away.
    Fools destroy themselves because of their indifference.

Proverbs 1:

So how will we escape punishment if we reject the important message, the message that God saved us?

Hebrews 2:3a

Be careful, brothers and sisters, that none of you ever develop a wicked, unbelieving heart that turns away from the living God.

Hebrews 3:12

Scripture says,
  "If you hear God speak today, don't be stubborn.
    Don't be stubborn like those who rebelled."

Hebrews 3:15

So remember what you received and heard. Obey, and change the way you think and act. If you're not alert, I'll come like a thief. You don't know when I will come.

Revelation 3:3

I know what you have done, that you are neither cold nor hot. I wish you were cold or hot.

Revelation 3:15

∾ INFATUATION ∾

Guard your heart more than anything else,
  because the source of your life flows from it.

Proverbs 4:23

My son,
    listen, be wise,
        and keep your mind going in the right direction.

Proverbs 23:1

The human mind is the most deceitful of all things. It is incurable.
    No one can understand how deceitful it is.

Jeremiah 17:

Dear children, we must show love through actions that are sincere, not
through empty words.

1 John 3:1

❧ INFERIORITY ❧

He places lowly people up high.
He lifts those who mourn to safety.

Job 5:1.

Even though the LORD is high above,
    he sees humble people ⌊close up⌋,
    and he recognizes arrogant people from a distance.

Psalm 138:

But many who are first will be last, and the last will be first.

Mark 10:3

At the same time the Spirit also helps us in our weakness, because we don't know how to pray for what we need. But the Spirit intercedes along with our groans that cannot be expressed in words.

Romans 8:26

God chose what the world considers ordinary and what it despises—what it considers to be nothing—in order to destroy what it considers to be something.

1 Corinthians 1:28

An eye can't say to a hand, "I don't need you!" Or again, the head can't say to the feet, "I don't need you!" The opposite is true. The parts of the body that we think are weaker are the ones we really need.

1 Corinthians 12:21-22

There are neither Jews nor Greeks, slaves nor free people, males nor females. You are all the same in Christ Jesus.

Galatians 3:28

Suppose you give special attention to the man wearing fine clothes and say to him, "Please have a seat." But you say to the poor man, "Stand over there," or "Sit on the floor at my feet." Aren't you discriminating against people and using a corrupt standard to make judgments?

James 2:3-4

❧ INSECURITY ❧

Those who know your name trust you, O LORD,
  because you have never deserted those who seek your help.

Psalm 9:1

The LORD will be your confidence.
He will keep your foot from getting caught.

Proverbs 3:2

In the fear of the LORD there is strong confidence,
  and his children will have a place of refuge.

Proverbs 14:2

What can we say about all of this? If God is for us, who can be against us?

Romans 8:3

The one who loves us gives us an overwhelming victory in all these difficulties.

Romans 8:3

I can do everything through Christ who strengthens me.

Philippians 4:1.

So we can confidently say,
   "The Lord is my helper.
      I will not be afraid.
         What can mortals do to me?"

Hebrews 13:6

❧ INSIGNIFICANCE ❧

When I look at your heavens,
   the creation of your fingers,
      the moon and the stars that you have set in place—
         what is a mortal that you remember him
            or the Son of Man that you take care of him?
      You have made him a little lower than yourself.
      You have crowned him with glory and honor.

Psalm 8:3-5

Guard me as if I were the pupil in your eye.
Hide me in the shadow of your wings.

Psalm 17:8

I will give thanks to you
   because I have been so amazingly and miraculously made.
      Your works are miraculous, and my soul is fully aware of this.

Psalm 139:14

How precious are your thoughts concerning me, O God!
How vast in number they are!
  If I try to count them,
    there would be more of them than there are grains of sand.

Psalm 139:17-18

Since you are precious to me, you are honored and I love you.
  I will exchange others for you.
    Nations will be the price I pay for your life.

Isaiah 43:4

I can guarantee this truth: Whatever you did for one of my brothers or
sisters, no matter how unimportant ₌they seemed₎, you did for me.

Matthew 25:40

❧ INSULTS ❧

"Because oppressed people are robbed and needy people groan,
  I will now arise," says the LORD.
  "I will provide safety for those who long for it."

Psalm 12:5

All who see me make fun of me.
  Insults pour from their mouths.
    They shake their heads and say,
      "Put yourself in the LORD's hands.

Let the LORD save him!
Let God rescue him since he is pleased with him!"

Psalm 22:7-8

Whoever corrects a mocker receives abuse.
Whoever warns a wicked person gets hurt.

Proverbs 9:7

When a stubborn fool is irritated, he shows it immediately,
   but a sensible person hides the insult.

Proverbs 12:16

But I tell you this: Love your enemies, and pray for those who persecute you. In this way you show that you are children of your Father in heaven. He makes his sun rise on people whether they are good or evil. He lets rain fall on them whether they are just or unjust.

Matthew 5:44-45

Therefore, I accept weakness, mistreatment, hardship, persecution, and difficulties suffered for Christ. It's clear that when I'm weak, I'm strong.

2 Corinthians 12:10

Christ never verbally abused those who verbally abused him. When he suffered, he didn't make any threats but left everything to the one who judges fairly.

1 Peter 2:23

Don't pay people back with evil for the evil they do to you, or ridicule those who ridicule you. Instead, bless them, because you were called to inherit a blessing.

1 Peter 3:9

❧ INTIMIDATION ❧

The LORD is my light and my salvation.
   Who is there to fear?
The LORD is my life's fortress.
   Who is there to be afraid of?

Psalm 27:1

God is our refuge and strength,
   an ever-present help in times of trouble.
That is why we are not afraid
   even when the earth quakes
      or the mountains topple into the depths of the sea.

Psalm 46:1-2

His heart is steady, and he is not afraid.
   In the end he will look triumphantly at his enemies.

Psalm 112:8

A person's fear sets a trap ⌊for him⌋,
   but one who trusts the LORD is safe.

Proverbs 29:25

I, Jeremiah, said, "Almighty LORD, I do not know how to speak. I am only a boy!"

But the LORD said to me, "Don't say that you are only a boy. You will go wherever I send you. You will say whatever I command you to say. Don't be afraid of people. I am with you, and I will rescue you," declares the LORD.

Jeremiah 1:6-8

Be alert. Be firm in the Christian faith. Be courageous and strong.

1 Corinthians 16:13

Also pray that God will give me the right words to say. Then I will speak boldly when I reveal the mystery of the Good News.

Ephesians 6:19

Don't let anyone look down on you for being young. Instead, make your speech, behavior, love, faith, and purity an example for other believers.

1 Timothy 4:12

❦ JEALOUSY ❧

"Never desire to take your neighbor's wife away from him.
"Never long for your neighbor's household, his field, his male or female slave, his ox, his donkey, or anything else that belongs to him."

Deuteronomy 5:21

Certainly, anger kills a stubborn fool,
  and jealousy murders a gullible person.

Job 5:2

Do not be preoccupied with evildoers.
Do not envy those who do wicked things.

Psalm 37:1

Surrender yourself to the LORD, and wait patiently for him.
  Do not be preoccupied with ⌊an evildoer⌋ who succeeds in his way
    when he carries out his schemes.

Psalm 37:7

A tranquil heart makes for a healthy body,
  but jealousy is ⌊like⌋ bone cancer.

Proverbs 14:30

When you are jealous and quarrel among yourselves, aren't you
influenced by your corrupt nature and living by human standards?

1 Corinthians 3:3b

Wherever there is jealousy and rivalry, there is disorder and every
kind of evil.

James 3:16

∾ JOY ∾

Don't be sad because the joy you have in the LORD is your strength.
Nehemiah 8:10b

In him our hearts find joy.
In his holy name we trust.

Psalm 33:21

Righteous people will find joy in the LORD and take refuge in him.
Everyone whose motives are decent will be able to brag.

Psalm 64:10

But let righteous people rejoice.
   Let them celebrate in God's presence.
   Let them overflow with joy.

Psalm 68:3

Come, let's sing joyfully to the LORD.
   Let's shout happily to the rock of our salvation.

Psalm 95:1

Let them bring songs of thanksgiving as their sacrifice.
Let them tell in joyful songs what he has done.

Psalm 107:22

Your written instructions are mine forever.
    They are the joy of my heart.

Psalm 119:111

May God, the source of hope, fill you with joy and peace through your faith in him. Then you will overflow with hope by the power of the Holy Spirit.

Romans 15:13

❧ KINDNESS OF GOD ❧

He gives great victories to his king.
He shows mercy to his anointed,
    to David, and to his descendant forever.

Psalm 18:50

"I hid my face from you for a moment in a burst of anger,
    but I will have compassion on you with everlasting kindness,"
        says the LORD your defender.

Isaiah 54:8

I will acknowledge the LORD's acts of mercy,
    and ⌊sing⌋ the praises of the LORD,
        because of everything that the LORD has done for us.
            He has done many good things for the nation of Israel
                because of his compassion and his unlimited mercy.

Isaiah 63:7

I led them with cords of human kindness, with ropes of love.
    I removed the yokes from their necks.
        I bent down and fed them.

Hosea 11:4

Rather, love your enemies, help them, and lend to them without expecting to get anything back. Then you will have a great reward. You will be the children of the Most High God. After all, he is kind to unthankful and evil people.

Luke 6:35

Do you have contempt for God, who is very kind to you, puts up with you, and deals patiently with you? Don't you realize that it is God's kindness that is trying to lead you to him and change the way you think and act?

Romans 2:4

Look at how kind and how severe God can be. He is severe to those who fell, but kind to you if you continue to hold on to his kindness.

Romans 11:22a

God has brought us back to life together with Christ Jesus and has given us a position in heaven with him. He did this through Christ Jesus out of his generosity to us in order to show his extremely rich kindness in the world to come.

Ephesians 2:6-7

However, when God our Savior made his kindness and love for humanity appear, he saved us, but not because of anything we had done to gain his approval. Instead, because of his mercy he saved us through the washing in which the Holy Spirit gives us new birth and renewal.

Titus 3:4-5

❧ KINGDOM OF GOD ❧

From then on, Jesus began to tell people, "Turn to God and change the way you think and act, because the kingdom of heaven is near!"

Matthew 4:17

I can guarantee that unless you live a life that has God's approval and do it more faithfully than the scribes and Pharisees, you will never enter the kingdom of heaven.

Matthew 5:20

But first, be concerned about his kingdom and what has his approval. Then all these things will be provided for you.

Matthew 6:33

I can guarantee this truth: Whoever doesn't receive the kingdom of God as a little child receives it will never enter it.

Mark 10:15

Don't be afraid, little flock. Your Father is pleased to give you the kingdom.

Luke 12:32

They can't say, "Here it is!" or "There it is!" You see, the kingdom of God is within you.

Luke 17:21

Jesus answered, "My kingdom doesn't belong to this world. If my kingdom belonged to this world, my followers would fight to keep me from being handed over to the Jews. My kingdom doesn't have its origin on earth."

John 18:36

God has rescued us from the power of darkness and has brought us into the kingdom of his Son, whom he loves.

Colossians 1:13

Therefore, we must be thankful that we have a kingdom that cannot be shaken. Because we are thankful, we must serve God with fear and awe in a way that pleases him.

Hebrews 12:28

∽ **KINDNESS** ∽

A person's anxiety will weigh him down,
    but an encouraging word makes him joyful.

Proverbs 12:25

Whoever despises his neighbor sins,
    but blessed is the one who is kind to humble people.

Proverbs 14:21

Love is patient. Love is kind. Love isn't jealous. It doesn't sing its own praises. It isn't arrogant.

1 Corinthians 13:4

But the spiritual nature produces love, joy, peace, patience, kindness, goodness, faithfulness.

Galatians 5:22

Be kind to each other, sympathetic, forgiving each other as God has forgiven you through Christ.

Ephesians 4:32

As holy people whom God has chosen and loved, be sympathetic, kind, humble, gentle, and patient.

Colossians 3:12

Make sure that no one ever pays back one wrong with another wrong. Instead, always try to do what is good for each other and everyone else.

1 Thessalonians 5:15

A servant of the Lord must not quarrel. Instead, he must be kind to everyone. He must be a good teacher. He must be willing to suffer wrong.

2 Timothy 2:24

⮞ LAZINESS ⮜

Lazy hands bring poverty,
    but hard-working hands bring riches.

Proverbs 10:4

Do not love sleep or you will end up poor.
Keep your eyes open, and you will have plenty to eat.

Proverbs 20:13

"Just a little sleep,
just a little slumber,
just a little nap."
    Then your poverty will come like a drifter,
        and your need will come like a bandit.

Proverbs 24:33-34

At last I have seen what is good and beautiful: It is to eat and drink and to enjoy the good in all our hard work under the sun during the brief lives God gives us. That is our lot ⌊in life⌋.

Ecclesiastes 5:18

Don't be lazy in showing your devotion. Use your energy to serve the Lord.

Romans 12:11

Our people should also learn how to set an example by doing good things when urgent needs arise so that they can live productive lives.

Titus 3:14

❧ LONELINESS ❧

Turn to me, and have pity on me.
   I am lonely and oppressed.

Psalm 25:16

God places lonely people in families.
   He leads prisoners out of prison into productive lives,
      but rebellious people must live in an unproductive land.

Psalm 68:6

Yet, I am always with you.
   You hold on to my right hand.

Psalm 73:23

Friends can destroy one another,
    but a loving friend can stick closer than family.

Proverbs 18:24

Jesus said . . . "And remember that I am always with you until the end of time."

Matthew 28:20b

But [Jesus] would go away to places where he could be alone for prayer.

Luke 5:16

I will not leave you all alone. I will come back to you.

John 14:18

≈ **LONGINGS** ≈

You gave him his heart's desire.
    You did not refuse the prayer from his lips.

Psalm 21:2

The LORD is my shepherd.
    I am never in need.

Psalm 23:1

You know all my desires, O Lord,
    and my groaning has not been hidden from you.

Psalm 38:9

As a deer longs for flowing streams,
   so my soul longs for you, O God.

Psalm 42:1

My soul longs and yearns
   for the LORD's courtyards.
My whole body shouts for joy to the living God.

Psalm 84:2

Delayed hope makes one sick at heart,
   but a fulfilled longing is a tree of life.

Proverbs 13:12

❧ LOVE OF GOD ❧

The LORD commands his mercy during the day,
   and at night his song is with me—
      a prayer to the God of my life.

Psalm 42:8

Because your mercy is as high as the heavens.
   Your truth reaches the skies.

Psalm 57:10

But you, O Lord, are a compassionate and merciful God.
   You are patient, always faithful and ready to forgive.

Psalm 86:15

The LORD appeared to me in a faraway place and said,
"I love you with an everlasting love.
So I will continue to show you my kindness."

Jeremiah 31:3

God loved the world this way: He gave his only Son so that everyone who believes in him will not die but will have eternal life.

John 3:16

"I have loved you the same way the Father has loved me. So live in my love."

John 15:9

Christ died for us while we were still sinners. This demonstrates God's love for us.

Romans 5:8

God has shown us his love by sending his only Son into the world so that we could have life through him.

1 John 4:9

We have known and believed that God loves us. God is love. Those who live in God's love live in God, and God lives in them.

1 John 4:16

❧ **MERCY** ❧

The LORD your God is a merciful God. He will not abandon you, destroy
you, or forget the promise to your ancestors that he swore he would keep.

Deuteronomy 4:31

Thank the LORD!
He has heard my prayer for mercy!

Psalm 28:6

He has not treated us as we deserve for our sins
or paid us back for our wrongs.

Psalm 103:10

But from everlasting to everlasting,
the LORD's mercy is on those who fear him.
His righteousness belongs
to their children and grandchildren.

Psalm 103:17

Blessed are those who show mercy.
They will be treated mercifully.

Matthew 5:7

Be merciful as your Father is merciful.

Luke 6:36

≈ MISTAKES ≈

Do not remember the sins of my youth or my rebellious ways.
   Remember me, O LORD, in keeping with your mercy
      and your goodness.

Psalm 25:7

Blessed is the person whose disobedience is forgiven
   and whose sin is pardoned.
Blessed is the person whom the LORD no longer accuses of sin
   and who has no deceitful thoughts.

Psalm 32:1-2

I made my sins known to you, and I did not cover up my guilt.
I decided to confess them to you, O LORD.
   Then you forgave all my sins.

Psalm 32:5

A person's steps are directed by the LORD,
   and the LORD delights in his way.
When he falls, he will not be thrown down headfirst
   because the LORD holds on to his hand.

Psalm 37:23-24

As far as the east is from the west—
   that is how far he has removed our rebellious acts from himself.

Psalm 103:12

O LORD, who would be able to stand
  if you kept a record of sins?
But with you there is forgiveness
  so that you can be feared.

Psalm 130:3-

As a dog goes back to its vomit,
  ⌊so⌋ a fool repeats his stupidity.

Proverbs 26:1

Whoever covers over his sins does not prosper.
Whoever confesses and abandons them receives compassion.

Proverbs 28:1

We know that all things work together for the good of those who love
God—those whom he has called according to his plan.

Romans 8:2

Put up with each other, and forgive each other if anyone has a
complaint. Forgive as the Lord forgave you.

Colossians 3:1

∽ MONEY ∽

Do not count on extortion ⌊to make you rich⌋.
Do not hope to gain anything through robbery.
    When riches increase, do not depend on them.

Psalm 62:10

No one can serve two masters. He will hate the first master and love the second, or he will be devoted to the first and despise the second. You cannot serve God and wealth.

Matthew 6:24

He told the people, "Be careful to guard yourselves from every kind of greed. Life is not about having a lot of material possessions."

Luke 12:15

Sell your material possessions, and give the money to the poor. Make yourselves wallets that don't wear out! Make a treasure for yourselves in heaven that never loses its value! In heaven thieves and moths can't get close enough to destroy your treasure.

Luke 12:33

We didn't bring anything into the world, and we can't take anything out of it. As long as we have food and clothes, we should be satisfied.
    But people who want to get rich keep falling into temptation. They are trapped by many stupid and harmful desires which drown them in

destruction and ruin. Certainly, the love of money is the root of all kinds of evil. Some people who have set their hearts on getting rich have wandered away from the Christian faith and have caused themselves a lot of grief.

1 Timothy 6:7-10

Don't love money. Be happy with what you have because God has said, "I will never abandon you or leave you."

Hebrews 13:5

⚮ MOTIVATION ⚮

And you, my son Solomon, learn to know your father's God. Serve the LORD wholeheartedly and willingly because he searches every heart and understands every thought ⌊we have⌋. If you dedicate your life to serving him, he will accept you. But if you abandon him, he will reject you from then on.

1 Chronicles 28:9

You have probed my heart.
You have confronted me at night.
You have tested me like silver,
    but you found nothing wrong.
I have determined that my mouth will not sin.

Psalm 17:3

The crucible is for refining silver and the smelter for gold,
   but the one who purifies hearts ⌊by fire⌋ is the LORD.

Proverbs 17:3

A person thinks everything he does is right,
   but the LORD weighs hearts.

Proverbs 21:2

The LORD Almighty is my strength.
   He makes my feet like those of a deer.
      He makes me walk on the mountains.

Habakkuk 3:19

Evil thoughts, murder, adultery, ⌊other⌋ sexual sins, stealing, lying, and cursing come from within.

Matthew 15:19

Don't act out of selfish ambition or be conceited. Instead, humbly think of others as being better than yourselves. Don't be concerned only about your own interests, but also be concerned about the interests of others.

Philippians 2:3-4

Brothers and sisters, I can't consider myself a winner yet. This is what I do: I don't look back, I lengthen my stride, and I run straight toward the goal to win the prize that God's heavenly call offers in Christ Jesus.

Whoever has a mature faith should think this way. And if you think differently, God will show you how to think.

Philippians 3:13-15

I can do everything through Christ who strengthens me.

Philippians 4:13

When you pray for things, you don't get them because you want them for the wrong reason—for your own pleasure.

James 4:3

❧ MOURNING ❧

I am worn out from my groaning.
My eyes flood my bed every night.
I soak my couch with tears.

Psalm 6:6

The LORD is near to those whose hearts are humble.
He saves those whose spirits are crushed.

Psalm 34:18

Morning, noon, and night I complain and groan,
   and he listens to my voice.

Psalm 55:17

Everything has its own time, and there is a specific time for every
activity under heaven: . . .
    a time to cry and
    a time to laugh,
    a time to mourn and
    a time to dance.

Ecclesiastes 3:1, 4

Then young women will rejoice and dance
    along with young men and old men.
I will turn their mourning into joy.
I will comfort them.
I will give them joy in place of their sorrow.

Jeremiah 31:13

Blessed are those who mourn.
    They will be comforted.

Matthew 5:4

Come to me, all who are tired from carrying heavy loads, and I will
give you rest.

Matthew 11:28

I'm leaving you peace. I'm giving you my peace. I don't give you the
kind of peace that the world gives. So don't be troubled or cowardly.

John 14:27

We know that all things work together for the good of those who love
God—those whom he has called according to his plan.

Romans 8:28

The lamb in the center near the throne will be their shepherd.
He will lead them to springs filled with the water of life,
    and God will wipe every tear from their eyes.

Revelation 7:17

He will wipe every tear from their eyes. There won't be any more
death. There won't be any grief, crying, or pain, because the first
things have disappeared.

Revelation 21:4

✌ NEGLECT ✌

It would be unthinkable for me to sin against the LORD by failing to
pray for you. I will go on teaching you the way that is good and right.

1 Samuel 12:23

Your laws make me happy.
I never forget your word.

Psalm 119:16

Poverty and shame come to a person who ignores discipline,
   but whoever pays attention
      to constructive criticism will be honored.

Proverbs 13:18

⌊Like⌋ a city broken into ⌊and⌋ left without a wall,
   ⌊so⌋ is a person who lacks self-control.

Proverbs 25:28

Whoever covers over his sins does not prosper.
Whoever confesses and abandons them receives compassion.

Proverbs 28:13

Let wicked people abandon their ways.
Let evil people abandon their thoughts.
Let them return to the LORD,
   and he will show compassion to them.
Let them return to our God,
   because he will freely forgive them.

Isaiah 55:7

How horrible it will be for you, scribes and Pharisees! You hypocrites!
You give ⌊God⌋ one-tenth of your mint, dill, and cumin. But you have
neglected justice, mercy, and faithfulness. These are the most
important things in Moses' Teachings. You should have done these
things without neglecting the others.

Matthew 23:23

We should not stop gathering together with other believers, as some of you are doing. Instead, we must continue to encourage each other even more as we see the day of the Lord coming.

Hebrews 10:25

Whoever knows what is right but doesn't do it is sinning.

James 4:17

❧ OVERWHELMED ❧

My guilt has overwhelmed me.
　　Like a heavy load, it is more than I can bear.

Psalm 38:4

My soul waits calmly for God alone.
　　My salvation comes from him.
He alone is my rock and my savior—my stronghold.
　　I cannot be severely shaken.

Psalm 62:1-2

Various sins overwhelm me.
　　You are the one who forgives our rebellious acts.

Psalm 65:3

Thanks be to the Lord,
    who daily carries our burdens for us.
        God is our salvation.

                                                    Psalm 68:19

I look up toward the mountains.
    Where can I find help?
My help comes from the LORD,
    the maker of heaven and earth.

                                                Psalm 121:1-2

Even though I walk into the middle of trouble,
    you guard my life against the anger of my enemies.
    You stretch out your hand,
        and your right hand saves me.

                                                Psalm 138:7

When you go through the sea, I am with you.
When you go through rivers, they will not sweep you away.
When you walk through fire, you will not be burned,
    and the flames will not harm you.

                                                  Isaiah 43:2

The LORD is good.
    ⌊He is⌋ a fortress in the day of trouble.
    He knows those who seek shelter in him.

                                                Nahum 1:7

In every way we're troubled, but we aren't crushed by our troubles. We're frustrated, but we don't give up. We're persecuted, but we're not abandoned. We're captured, but we're not killed.

2 Corinthians 4:8-9

Never worry about anything. But in every situation let God know what you need in prayers and requests while giving thanks. Then God's peace, which goes beyond anything we can imagine, will guard your thoughts and emotions through Christ Jesus.

Philippians 4:6-7

Jesus Christ is the same yesterday, today, and forever.

Hebrews 13:8

✎ **PAIN** ✎

Even though I walk through the dark valley of death,
    because you are with me, I fear no harm.
        Your rod and your staff give me courage.

Psalm 23:4

This is my comfort in my misery:
    Your promise gave me a new life.

Psalm 119:50

Let your mercy comfort me
as you promised.

Psalm 119:76

He is the healer of the brokenhearted.
He is the one who bandages their wounds.

Psalm 147:3

Blessed are those who mourn.
They will be comforted.

Matthew 5:4

Come to me, all who are tired from carrying heavy loads, and I will
give you rest.

Matthew 11:28

I am convinced that nothing can ever separate us from God's love
which Christ Jesus our Lord shows us. We can't be separated by death
or life, by angels or rulers, by anything in the present or anything in
the future, by forces or powers in the world above or in the world
below, or by anything else in creation.

Romans 8:38-39

He comforts us whenever we suffer. That is why whenever other
people suffer, we are able to comfort them by using the same comfort
we have received from God.

2 Corinthians 1:4

That is why we are not discouraged. Though outwardly we are wearing out, inwardly we are renewed day by day.

2 Corinthians 4:16

We don't enjoy being disciplined. It always seems to cause more pain than joy. But later on, those who learn from that discipline have peace that comes from doing what is right.

Hebrews 12:11

God is pleased if a person is aware of him while enduring the pains of unjust suffering.

1 Peter 2:19

Dear friends, don't be surprised by the fiery troubles that are coming in order to test you. Don't feel as though something strange is happening to you, but be happy as you share Christ's sufferings. Then you will also be full of joy when he appears again in his glory.

1 Peter 4:12

✌ PANIC ✌

Listen, Israel, today you're going into battle against your enemies. Don't lose your courage! Don't be afraid or alarmed or tremble because of them.

Deuteronomy 20:3

I called on the LORD in my distress.
  I cried to my God for help.
    He heard my voice from his temple,
      and my cry for help reached his ears.

Psalm 18:6

The LORD will answer you in times of trouble.
The name of the God of Jacob will protect you.

Psalm 20:1

⌊The LORD says,⌋
  "I will instruct you.
  I will teach you the way that you should go.
  I will advise you as my eyes watch over you.

Psalm 32:8

God is our refuge and strength,
  an ever-present help in times of trouble.
That is why we are not afraid
  even when the earth quakes
    or the mountains topple into the depths of the sea.

Psalm 46:1-2

Let go ⌊of your concerns⌋!
  Then you will know that I am God.

I rule the nations.
I rule the earth.

Psalm 46:10

Trust the LORD with all your heart,
    and do not rely on your own understanding.
In all your ways acknowledge him,
    and he will make your paths smooth.

Proverbs 3:5-6

Do not be afraid of sudden terror
    or of the destruction of wicked people when it comes.

Proverbs 3:25

Don't be afraid, because I am with you.
Don't be intimidated; I am your God.
    I will strengthen you.
    I will help you.
    I will support you with my victorious right hand.

Isaiah 41:10

I know the plans that I have for you, declares the LORD. They are plans
for peace and not disaster, plans to give you a future filled with hope.

Jeremiah 29:11

You haven't received the spirit of slaves that leads you into fear again. Instead, you have received the spirit of God's adopted children by which we call out, "Abba! Father!"

Romans 8:15

God didn't give us a cowardly spirit but a spirit of power, love, and good judgment.

2 Timothy 1:7

∽ PATIENCE ∽

Wait with hope for the LORD.
Be strong, and let your heart be courageous.
Yes, wait with hope for the LORD.

Psalm 27:14

Surrender yourself to the LORD, and wait patiently for him.
Do not be preoccupied with ⌊an evildoer⌋ who succeeds in his way
when he carries out his schemes.

Psalm 37:7

A person with good sense is patient,
and it is to his credit that he overlooks an offense.

Proverbs 19:11

"Listen now, descendants of David," Isaiah said. "Isn't it enough that you try the patience of mortals? Must you also try the patience of my God?

Isaiah 7:13

But the person who endures to the end will be saved.

Matthew 24:13

We encourage you, brothers and sisters, to instruct those who are not living right, cheer up those who are discouraged, help the weak, and be patient with everyone.

1 Thessalonians 5:14

However, I was treated with mercy so that Christ Jesus could use me, the foremost sinner, to demonstrate his patience. This patience serves as an example for those who would believe in him and live forever.

1 Timothy 1:16

You, too, must be patient. Don't give up hope. The Lord will soon be here.

James 5:8

What credit do you deserve if you endure a beating for doing something wrong? But if you endure suffering for doing something good, God is pleased with you.

1 Peter 2:20

The Lord isn't slow to do what he promised, as some people think. Rather, he is patient for your sake. He doesn't want to destroy anyone but wants all people to have an opportunity to turn to him and change the way they think and act.

2 Peter 3:9

❧ PEACE ❧

I fall asleep in peace the moment I lie down
   because you alone, O LORD, enable me to live securely.

Psalm 4:8

The LORD will give power to his people.
The LORD will bless his people with peace.

Psalm 29:11

Let go ⌊of your concerns⌋!
   Then you will know that I am God.
      I rule the nations.
      I rule the earth.

Psalm 46:10

A child will be born for us.
A son will be given to us.
   The government will rest on his shoulders.
   He will be named:

Wonderful Counselor,
Mighty God,
Everlasting Father,
Prince of Peace.

Isaiah 9:6

With perfect peace you will protect
those whose minds cannot be changed,
because they trust you.

Isaiah 26:3

Don't be troubled. Believe in God.

John 14:1a

I'm leaving you peace. I'm giving you my peace. I don't give you the kind of peace that the world gives. So don't be troubled or cowardly.

John 14:27

Now that we have God's approval by faith, we have peace with God because of what our Lord Jesus Christ has done.

Romans 5:1

In every way we're troubled, but we aren't crushed by our troubles. We're frustrated, but we don't give up. We're persecuted, but we're not abandoned. We're captured, but we're not killed.

2 Corinthians 4:8-9

Also, let Christ's peace control you. God has called you into this peace
by bringing you into one body. Be thankful.

Colossians 3:15

⚖ PEACEMAKERS ⚖

Notice the innocent person,
   and look at the decent person,
      because the peacemaker has a future.

Psalm 37:37

See how good and pleasant it is
   when brothers and sisters live together in harmony!

Psalm 133:1

Blessed are those who make peace.
   They will be called God's children.

Matthew 5:9

Through the peace that ties you together, do your best to maintain the
unity that the Spirit gives.

Ephesians 4:3

Believers shouldn't curse anyone or be quarrelsome, but they should
be gentle and show courtesy to everyone.

Titus 3:2

Try to live peacefully with everyone, and try to live holy lives, because if you don't, you will not see the Lord.

Hebrews 12:14

A harvest that has God's approval comes from the peace planted by peacemakers.

James 3:18

Finally, everyone must live in harmony, be sympathetic, love each other, have compassion, and be humble.

1 Peter 3:8

People who want to live a full life and enjoy good days
   must keep their tongues from saying evil things. . . .
They must turn away from evil and do good.
   They must seek peace and pursue it.

1 Peter 3:10-11

❧ PEER PRESSURE ❧

Blessed is the person who does not
   follow the advice of wicked people,
      take the path of sinners,
         or join the company of mockers.

Psalm 1:1

My son,
  if sinners lure you, do not go along.

Proverbs 1:10

Do not envy evil people
  or wish you were with them.

Proverbs 24:1

Don't let anyone deceive you. Associating with bad people will ruin decent people.

1 Corinthians 15:33

We demonstrate that we are God's servants as we are praised and dishonored, as we are slandered and honored, and as we use what is right to attack what is wrong and to defend the truth. We are treated as dishonest although we are honest.

2 Corinthians 6:7b-8

Am I saying this now to win the approval of people or God? Am I trying to please people? If I were still trying to please people, I would not be Christ's servant.

Galatians 1:10

⊷ **PERSECUTION** ⊶

"Because oppressed people are robbed and needy people groan,
    I will now arise," says the LORD.
"I will provide safety for those who long for it."

Psalm 12:5

You hide them in the secret place of your presence
    from those who scheme against them.
You keep them in a shelter,
    safe from quarrelsome tongues.

Psalm 31:20

From the time I was young, people have attacked me,
    but they have never overpowered me.

Psalm 129:2

The reason I can ⌊still⌋ find hope is that I keep this one thing in mind:
the LORD's mercy.
    We were not completely wiped out.
    His compassion is never limited.
        It is new every morning.
        His faithfulness is great.

Lamentations 3:21-23

The LORD your God is with you.
>He is a hero who saves you.
>>He happily rejoices over you,
>>>renews you with his love,
>>>>and celebrates over you with shouts of joy.

Zephaniah 3:17b

Blessed are those who are persecuted
>for doing what God approves of.
>The kingdom of heaven belongs to them.

Matthew 5:10

The person who hears you hears me, and the person who rejects you rejects me. The person who rejects me rejects the one who sent me.

Luke 10:16

Those who try to live a godly life because they believe in Christ Jesus will be persecuted.

2 Timothy 3:12

God is fair. He won't forget what you've done or the love you've shown for him.

Hebrews 6:10a

If you are insulted because of the name of Christ, you are blessed because the Spirit of glory—the Spirit of God—is resting on you.

1 Peter 4:14

If you suffer for being a Christian, don't feel ashamed, but praise God for being called that name.

1 Peter 4:1

❧ PERSEVERANCE ❧

My steps have remained firmly in your paths.
My feet have not slipped.

Psalm 17:

The Almighty LORD helps me.
    That is why I will not be ashamed.
      I have set my face like a flint.
        I know that I will not be put to shame.

Isaiah 50:

He will give everlasting life to those who search for glory, honor, and immortality by persisting in doing what is good.

Romans 2:

So, then, brothers and sisters, don't let anyone move you off the foundation ⌊of your faith⌋. Always excel in the work you do for the Lord. You know that the hard work you do for the Lord is not pointless.

1 Corinthians 15:5

We can't allow ourselves to get tired of living the right way. Certainly, each of us will receive ⌊everlasting life⌋ at the proper time, if we don't give up.

Galatians 6:9

May the Lord direct your lives as you show God's love and Christ's endurance.

2 Thessalonians 3:5

Brothers and sisters, we can't allow ourselves to get tired of doing what is right.

2 Thessalonians 3:13

I have fought the good fight. I have completed the race. I have kept the faith.

2 Timothy 4:7

Endure until your testing is over. Then you will be mature and complete, and you won't need anything.

James 1:4

Blessed are those who endure when they are tested. When they pass the test, they will receive the crown of life that God has promised to those who love him.

James 1:12

✎ PESSIMISM ✎

Even though an army sets up camp against me,
  my heart will not be afraid.
Even though a war breaks out against me,
  I will still have confidence ⌊in the LORD⌋.

Psalm 27:3

Wait with hope for the LORD.
Be strong, and let your heart be courageous.
Yes, wait with hope for the LORD.

Psalm 27:14

Be strong, all who wait with hope for the LORD,
  and let your heart be courageous.

Psalm 31:24

Why are you discouraged, my soul?
Why are you so restless?
  Put your hope in God,
    because I will still praise him.
      He is my savior and my God.

Psalm 42:5

"The mountains may move, and the hills may shake,
  but my kindness will never depart from you.

My promise of peace will never change,"
    says the LORD, who has compassion on you.

Isaiah 54:10

I will not leave you all alone. I will come back to you.

John 14:18

We know that all things work together for the good of those who love
God—those whom he has called according to his plan.

Romans 8:28

Glory belongs to God, whose power is at work in us. By this power he
can do infinitely more than we can ask or imagine.

Ephesians 3:20

Therefore, your minds must be clear and ready for action. Place your
confidence completely in what God's kindness will bring you when
Jesus Christ appears again.

1 Peter 1:13

✇ POWER ✇

The LORD is my light and my salvation.
    Who is there to fear?
The LORD is my life's fortress.
    Who is there to be afraid of?

Psalm 27:1

Say to God,
  "How awe-inspiring are your deeds!
  Your power is so great
      that your enemies will cringe in front of you."

Psalm 66:3

When I called, you answered me.
  You made me bold by strengthening my soul.

Psalm 138:3

Our Lord is great, and his power is great.
There is no limit to his understanding.

Psalm 147:5

Praise him for his mighty acts.
Praise him for his immense greatness.

Psalm 150:2

You won't ⌊succeed⌋ by might or by power, but by my Spirit, says the
LORD of Armies.

Zechariah 4:6b

But you will receive power when the Holy Spirit comes to you. Then
you will be my witnesses to testify about me in Jerusalem, throughout
Judea and Samaria, and to the ends of the earth.

Acts 1:8

I'm not ashamed of the Good News. It is God's power to save everyone who believes, Jews first and Greeks as well.

Romans 1:16

At the same time the Spirit also helps us in our weakness, because we don't know how to pray for what we need. But the Spirit intercedes along with our groans that cannot be expressed in words. The one who searches our hearts knows what the Spirit has in mind. The Spirit intercedes for God's people the way God wants him to.

Romans 8:26-27

God's kingdom is not just talk, it is power.

1 Corinthians 4:20

Since you want proof that Christ is speaking through me, that's what you'll get. Christ isn't weak in dealing with you. Instead, he makes his power felt among you.

2 Corinthians 13:3

You will also know the unlimited greatness of his power as it works with might and strength for us, the believers.

Ephesians 1:19

Our Lord and God, you deserve to receive glory, honor, and power
    because you created everything.
Everything came into existence and was created
    because of your will.

Revelation 4:11

❧ PRAYER ❧

You will pray to him, and he will listen to you,
    and you will keep your vow to him.

Job 22:27

Call on me in times of trouble.
    I will rescue you, and you will honor me.

Psalm 50:15

Entrust your efforts to the LORD,
    and your plans will succeed.

Proverbs 16:3

Before they call, I will answer.
While they're still speaking, I will hear.

Isaiah 65:24

When you pray, go to your room and close the door. Pray privately to
your Father who is with you. Your Father sees what you do in private.
He will reward you.

Matthew 6:6

Don't be like them. Your Father knows what you need before you
ask him.

Matthew 6:8

Ask, and you will receive. Search, and you will find. Knock, and the door will be opened for you. Everyone who asks will receive. The one who searches will find, and for the one who knocks, the door will be opened.

Matthew 7:7-8

At that time Jesus went to a mountain to pray. He spent the whole night in prayer to God.

Luke 6:12

Pray in the Spirit in every situation. Use every kind of prayer and request there is. For the same reason be alert. Use every kind of effort and make every kind of request for all of God's people.

Ephesians 6:18

Never stop praying.

1 Thessalonians 5:17

First of all, I encourage you to make petitions, prayers, intercessions, and prayers of thanks for all people.

1 Timothy 2:1

So admit your sins to each other, and pray for each other so that you will be healed.
Prayers offered by those who have God's approval are effective.

James 5:16

❦ PRESSURE ❦

I went to the LORD for help.
   He answered me and rescued me from all my fears.

Psalm 34:4

Turn your burdens over to the LORD,
   and he will take care of you.
      He will never let the righteous person stumble.

Psalm 55:22

Thanks be to the Lord,
   who daily carries our burdens for us.
      God is our salvation.

Psalm 68:19

O LORD, listen to my prayer.
   Open your ears to hear my urgent requests.
   Answer me because you are faithful and righteous.

Psalm 143:1

Don't be afraid, because I am with you.
Don't be intimidated; I am your God.
   I will strengthen you.
   I will help you.
   I will support you with my victorious right hand.

Isaiah 41:10

We were not completely wiped out.
His compassion is never limited.
   It is new every morning.
   His faithfulness is great.

Lamentations 3:22-23

Water flowed over my head. I thought I was finished.
"I call your name from the deepest pit, O LORD.
   Listen to my cry ⌊for help⌋.
   Don't close your ears when I cry out for relief."

Lamentations 3:54,56

Don't become like the people of this world. Instead, change the way you think. Then you will always be able to determine what God really wants—what is good, pleasing, and perfect.

Romans 12:2

In every way we're troubled, but we aren't crushed by our troubles. We're frustrated, but we don't give up.

2 Corinthians 4:8

Blessed are those who endure when they are tested. When they pass the test, they will receive the crown of life that God has promised to those who love him.

James 1:12

❧ **PROBLEMS** ❧

But trouble comes to you, and you're impatient.
  It touches you, and you panic.

Job 4:5

But a person is born for trouble as surely as sparks fly up ⌊from a fire⌋.
Job 5:7

Countless evils have surrounded me.
  My sins have caught up with me so that I can no longer see.
    They outnumber the hairs on my head.
      I have lost heart.

Psalm 40:12

God is our refuge and strength,
  an ever-present help in times of trouble.

Psalm 46:1

When I am in trouble, I call out to you
  because you answer me.

Psalm 86:7

I look up toward the mountains.
  Where can I find help?

My help comes from the LORD,
    the maker of heaven and earth.

Psalm 121:1-2

Even though I walk into the middle of trouble,
    you guard my life against the anger of my enemies.
    You stretch out your hand,
        and your right hand saves me.

Psalm 138:7

ertainly, it is right for God to give suffering to those who cause you to
ffer. It is also right for God to give all of us relief from our suffering.
e will do this when the Lord Jesus is revealed, ⌊coming⌋ from heaven
ith his mighty angels in a blazing fire.

2 Thessalonians 1:6-7

any of you are having trouble, pray. If you are happy, sing psalms.

James 5:13

PURITY

You have probed my heart.
You have confronted me at night.
You have tested me like silver,
    but you found nothing wrong.
I have determined that my mouth will not sin.

Psalm 17:3

The LORD paid me back
  because of my righteousness,
  because he can see that my hands are clean.

Psalm 18

I made my sins known to you, and I did not cover up my guilt.
I decided to confess them to you, O LORD.
  Then you forgave all my sins.

Psalm 3.

Create a clean heart in me, O God,
  and renew a faithful spirit within me.

Psalm 51.

God is truly good to Israel,
  to those whose lives are pure.

Psalm 7

Blessed are those whose thoughts are pure.
  They will see God.

Matthew

Because all people have sinned, they have fallen short of God's glory. The
receive God's approval freely by an act of his kindness through the price
Christ Jesus paid to set us free ₁from sin₎.

Romans 3:23

nally, brothers and sisters, keep your thoughts on whatever is right or
serves praise: things that are true, honorable, fair, pure, acceptable, or
mmendable.

Philippians 4:8

arriage is honorable in every way, so husbands and wives should be
thful to each other. God will judge those who commit sexual sins,
pecially those who commit adultery.

Hebrews 13:4

t if we live in the light in the same way that God is in the light, we have a
lationship with each other. And the blood of his Son Jesus cleanses us
m every sin.

1 John 1:7

thing unclean, no one who does anything detestable, and no liars will
er enter it. Only those whose names are written in the lamb's Book of
e will enter it.

Revelation 21:27

∽ RELIEF ∾

He reached down from high above and took hold of me.
He pulled me out of the raging water.

Psalm 18:16

I will rejoice and be glad because of your mercy.
    You have seen my misery.
    You have known the troubles in my soul.

Psalm 3

In their distress they cried out to the LORD.
    He rescued them from their troubles.

Psalm 10

You saved me from death.
You saved my eyes from tears ⌊and⌋ my feet from stumbling.

Psalm 11

I am drowning in tears.
    Strengthen me as you promised.

Psalm 119.

O LORD, listen to my prayer.
    Open your ears to hear my urgent requests.
    Answer me because you are faithful and righteous.

Psalm 14

Come to me, all who are tired from carrying heavy loads, and I will give you rest.

Matthew 11:

e will wipe every tear from their eyes. There won't be any more
eath. There won't be any grief, crying, or pain, because the first
ings have disappeared.

Revelation 21:4

❧ **RESENTFULNESS** ❧

Do not reject the discipline of the LORD, my son,
   and do not resent his warning.

Proverbs 3:11

A mocker does not appreciate a warning.
   He will not go to wise people.

Proverbs 15:12

A person with good sense is patient,
   and it is to his credit that he overlooks an offense.

Proverbs 19:11

A fool expresses all his emotions,
   but a wise person controls them.

Proverbs 29:11

can see that you are bitter with jealousy and wrapped up in your evil
ays.

Acts 8:23

Each of you should give whatever you have decided. You shouldn't be
sorry that you gave or feel forced to give, since God loves a cheerful
giver.

2 Corinthians 9

Get rid of your bitterness, hot tempers, anger, loud quarreling,
cursing, and hatred. Be kind to each other, sympathetic, forgiving eac
other as God has forgiven you through Christ.

Ephesians 4:31-

A servant of the Lord must not quarrel. Instead, he must be kind to
everyone. He must be a good teacher. He must be willing to suffer
wrong.

2 Timothy 2.

Brothers and sisters, stop complaining about each other, or you will b
condemned.

James 5:

✑ REST ✑

By the seventh day God had finished the work he had been doing. On
the seventh day he stopped the work he had been doing.

Genesis

The LORD's beloved people will live securely with him.
    The LORD will shelter them all day long.

Deuteronomy 33:12b

I fall asleep in peace the moment I lie down
    because you alone, O LORD, enable me to live securely.

Psalm 4:8

He renews my soul.
He guides me along the paths of righteousness
    for the sake of his name.

Psalm 23:3

I waited patiently for the LORD.
    He turned to me and heard my cry for help.
    He pulled me out of a horrible pit,
        out of the mud and clay.
    He set my feet on a rock
        and made my steps secure.
    He placed a new song in my mouth,
        a song of praise to our God.
            Many will see this and worship.
            They will trust the LORD.

Psalm 40:1-3

Wait calmly for God alone, my soul,
    because my hope comes from him.

Psalm 62:5

Come to me, all who are tired from carrying heavy loads, and I will
give you rest.

Matthew 11:28

❧ RISK-TAKING ❧

I have commanded you, "Be strong and courageous! Don't tremble or
be terrified, because the LORD your God is with you wherever you go."

Joshua 1:9

When I called, you answered me.
    You made me bold by strengthening my soul.

Psalm 138:3

A wicked person flees when no one is chasing him,
    but righteous people are as bold as lions.

Proverbs 28:1

Those who want to save their lives will lose them. But those who lose
their lives for me will find them.

Matthew 16:25

Lord, pay attention to their threats now, and allow us to speak your word boldly.

Acts 4:29

But he told me: "My kindness is all you need. My power is strongest when you are weak." So I will brag even more about my weaknesses in order that Christ's power will live in me.

2 Corinthians 12:9

It's far more than that! I consider everything else worthless because I'm much better off knowing Christ Jesus my Lord. It's because of him that I think of everything as worthless. I threw it all away in order to gain Christ

Philippians 3:8

As you know, we suffered rough and insulting treatment in Philippi. But our God gave us the courage to tell you his Good News in spite of strong opposition.

1 Thessalonians 2:2

So we can confidently say,
    "The Lord is my helper.
        I will not be afraid.
            What can mortals do to me?"

Hebrews 13:6

❧ SADNESS ❧

You have seen ⌊it⌋; yes, you have taken note of trouble and grief
   and placed them under your control.
      The victim entrusts himself to you.
You alone have been the helper of orphans.

Psalm 10:14

O LORD, you light my lamp.
   My God turns my darkness into light.

Psalm 18:28

I am poured out like water,
   and all my bones are out of joint.
      My heart is like wax.
         It has melted within me.

Psalm 22:14

Even though I walk through the dark valley of death,
   because you are with me, I fear no harm.
      Your rod and your staff give me courage.

Psalm 23:4

Have pity on me, O LORD, because I am in distress.
   My eyes, my soul, and my body waste away from grief.

Psalm 31:9

The LORD is near to those whose hearts are humble.
He saves those whose spirits are crushed.

Psalm 34:18

I am drowning in tears.
Strengthen me as you promised.

Psalm 119:28

He is the healer of the brokenhearted.
He is the one who bandages their wounds.

Psalm 147:3

He was despised and rejected by people.
He was a man of sorrows, familiar with suffering.
He was despised like one from whom people turn their faces,
and we didn't consider him to be worth anything.

Isaiah 53:3

In fact, we still feel as if we're under a death sentence. But we suffered
so that we would stop trusting ourselves and learn to trust God, who
brings the dead back to life.

2 Corinthians 1:9

He will wipe every tear from their eyes. There won't be any more
death. There won't be any grief, crying, or pain, because the first
things have disappeared.

Revelation 21:4

❧ SAFETY ❧

But you, O LORD, are a shield that surrounds me.
    You are my glory.
    You hold my head high.

Psalm 3:3

I fall asleep in peace the moment I lie down
    because you alone, O LORD, enable me to live securely.

Psalm 4:8

Protect me, O God, because I take refuge in you.

Psalm 16:1

The LORD is my rock and my fortress and my Savior,
    my God, my rock in whom I take refuge,
        my shield, and the strength of my salvation,
            my stronghold.

Psalm 18:2

He hides me in his shelter when there is trouble.
He keeps me hidden in his tent.
He sets me high on a rock.

Psalm 27:5

He will put his angels in charge of you
   to protect you in all your ways.

Psalm 91:11

He is our God
   and we are the people in his care,
      the flock that he leads.

Psalm 95:7a

During times of trouble I called on the LORD.
   The LORD answered me ⌊and⌋ set me free ⌊from all of them⌋.
The LORD is on my side.
   I am not afraid.
      What can mortals do to me?

Psalm 118:5-6

O LORD, you have examined me, and you know me.
   You alone know when I sit down and when I get up.
   You read my thoughts from far away. . . .
   You are all around me—in front of me and in back of me.
   You lay your hand on me.

Psalm 139:1-2, 5

When you go through the sea, I am with you.
When you go through rivers, they will not sweep you away.

When you walk through fire, you will not be burned,
    and the flames will not harm you.

Isaiah 43:2

Aren't five sparrows sold for two cents? God doesn't forget any of them. Even every hair on your head has been counted. Don't be afraid! You are worth more than many sparrows.

Luke 12:6-7

I'm not asking you to take them out of the world but to protect them from the evil one.

John 17:15

We know that those who have been born from God don't go on sinning. Rather, the Son of God protects them, and the evil one can't harm them.

1 John 5:18

❧ SATISFACTION ❧

Naked I came from my mother,
    and naked I will return.
The LORD has given,
    and the LORD has taken away!
May the name of the LORD be praised.

Job 1:21

You are my Lord. Without you, I have nothing good.

Psalm 16:2

Oppressed people will eat until they are full.
Those who look to the LORD will praise him.
  May you live forever.

Psalm 22:26

You open your hand,
  and you satisfy the desire of every living thing.

Psalm 145:16

A lazy person craves food and there is none,
  but the appetite of hard-working people is satisfied.

Proverbs 13:4

Whoever loves money will never be satisfied with money. Whoever
loves wealth will never be satisfied with more income. Even this is
pointless.

Ecclesiastes 5:10

Why do you spend money on what cannot nourish you
  and your wages on what does not satisfy you?
Listen carefully to me:
  Eat what is good, and enjoy the best foods.

Isaiah 55:2

Jesus answered her, "Everyone who drinks this water will become thirsty again. But those who drink the water that I will give them will never become thirsty again. In fact, the water I will give them will become in them a spring that gushes up to eternal life."

John 4:13-14

Jesus told them, "I am the bread of life. Whoever comes to me will never become hungry, and whoever believes in me will never become thirsty."

John 6:35

I'm not saying this because I'm in any need. I've learned to be content in whatever situation I'm in. I know how to live in poverty or prosperity. No matter what the situation, I've learned the secret of how to live when I'm full or when I'm hungry, when I have too much or when I have too little.

Philippians 4:11-12

A godly life brings huge profits to people who are content with what they have.

1 Timothy 6:6

God's divine power has given us everything we need for life and for godliness. This power was given to us through knowledge of the one who called us by his own glory and integrity.

2 Peter 1:3

∽ SECOND COMING ∽ OF CHRIST

The Son of Man will come with his angels in his Father's glory. Then he will pay back each person based on what that person has done.

Matthew 16:27

This Good News about the kingdom will be spread throughout the world as a testimony to all nations. Then the end will come.

Matthew 24:14

Be ready, because the Son of Man will return when you least expect him.

Luke 12:40

My Father's house has many rooms. If that were not true, would I have told you that I'm going to prepare a place for you? If I go to prepare a place for you, I will come again. Then I will bring you into my presence so that you will be where I am.

John 14:2-3

They asked, "Why are you men from Galilee standing here looking at the sky? Jesus, who was taken from you to heaven, will come back in the same way that you saw him go to heaven."

Acts 1:11

I'm telling you a mystery. Not all of us will die, but we will all be changed. It will happen in an instant, in a split second at the sound of the last trumpet. Indeed, that trumpet will sound, and then the dead will come back to life. They will be changed so that they can live forever.

1 Corinthians 15:51-52

The Lord will come from heaven with a command, with the voice of the archangel, and with the trumpet ⌊call⌋ of God. First, the dead who believed in Christ will come back to life. Then, together with them, we who are still alive will be taken in the clouds to meet the Lord in the air. In this way we will always be with the Lord.

1 Thessalonians 4:16-17

The day of the Lord will come like a thief. On that day heaven will pass away with a roaring sound. Everything that makes up the universe will burn and be destroyed. The earth and everything that people have done on it will be exposed.

2 Peter 3:10

But we look forward to what God has promised—a new heaven and a new earth—a place where everything that has God's approval lives.

2 Peter 3:13

Dear friends, now we are God's children. What we will be isn't completely clear yet. We do know that when Christ appears we will be like him because we will see him as he is.

1 John 3:2

∽ SECURITY ∽

The eternal God is your shelter,
    and his everlasting arms support you.
He will force your enemies out of your way
    and tell you to destroy them.

Deuteronomy 33:27

The LORD is my rock and my fortress and my Savior,
    my God, my rock in whom I take refuge,
        my shield, and the strength of my salvation,
            my stronghold.

Psalm 18:2

Even though an army sets up camp against me,
    my heart will not be afraid.
Even though a war breaks out against me,
    I will still have confidence ⌊in the LORD⌋.

Psalm 27:3

You are my hiding place.
You protect me from trouble.
You surround me with joyous songs of salvation.

Psalm 32:7

He pulled me out of a horrible pit,
    out of the mud and clay.
He set my feet on a rock
    and made my steps secure.

Psalm 40:2

God is our refuge and strength,
    an ever-present help in times of trouble.

Psalm 46:1

You, O LORD, are my refuge!
You have made the Most High your home.
    No harm will come to you.
    No sickness will come near your house.

Psalm 91:9-10

His heart is steady, and he is not afraid.
    In the end he will look triumphantly at his enemies.

Psalm 112:8

The name of the LORD is a strong tower.
    A righteous person runs to it and is safe.

Proverbs 18:10

I give them eternal life. They will never be lost, and no one will tear them away from me.

John 10:28

In every way we're troubled, but we aren't crushed by our troubles. We're frustrated, but we don't give up. We're persecuted, but we're not abandoned. We're captured, but we're not killed.

2 Corinthians 4:8-9

We have this confidence as a sure and strong anchor for our lives.

Hebrews 6:19a

∼ SELFISHNESS ∼

Direct my heart toward your written instructions
   rather than getting rich in underhanded ways.

Psalm 119:36

No one can serve two masters. He will hate the first master and love the second, or he will be devoted to the first and despise the second. You cannot serve God and wealth.

Matthew 6:24

Then Jesus said to his disciples, "Those who want to come with me must say no to the things they want, pick up their crosses, and follow me."

Matthew 16:24

Whoever wants to be the most important person must take the last place and be a servant to everyone else.

Mark 9:35b

He told the people, "Be careful to guard yourselves from every kind of greed. Life is not about having a lot of material possessions."

Luke 12:15

Because of the kindness that God has shown me, I ask you not to think of yourselves more highly than you should.

Romans 12:3a

It's clear that we don't live to honor ourselves, and we don't die to honor ourselves.

Romans 14:7

People should be concerned about others and not just about themselves.

1 Corinthians 10:24

[Love] isn't rude. It doesn't think about itself. It isn't irritable. It doesn't keep track of wrongs.

1 Corinthians 13:5

He died for all people so that those who live should no longer live for themselves but for the man who died and was brought back to life for them.

2 Corinthians 5:15

Don't act out of selfish ambition or be conceited. Instead, humbly think of others as being better than yourselves.

Philippians 2:3

We didn't bring anything into the world, and we can't take anything out of it. As long as we have food and clothes, we should be satisfied.

But people who want to get rich keep falling into temptation. They are trapped by many stupid and harmful desires which drown them in destruction and ruin. Certainly, the love of money is the root of all kinds of evil. Some people who have set their hearts on getting rich have wandered away from the Christian faith and have caused themselves a lot of grief.

1 Timothy 6:7-10

Wherever there is jealousy and rivalry, there is disorder and every kind of evil.

James 3:16

∽ **SERVICE** ∽

The LORD protects the souls of his servants.
All who take refuge in him will never be condemned.

Psalm 34:22

Who's the greatest, the person who sits at the table or the servant?
Isn't it really the person who sits at the table? But I'm among you as a
servant.

Luke 22:27

Serve eagerly as if you were serving your heavenly master and not
merely serving human masters.

Ephesians 6:7

[Jesus Christ] emptied himself by taking on the form of a servant,
     by becoming like other humans,
     by having a human appearance.

Philippians 2:7

Whatever you do, do it wholeheartedly as though you were working
for your real master and not merely for humans. You know that your
real master will give you an inheritance as your reward. It is Christ,
your real master, whom you are serving.

Colossians 3:23-24

❧ SHAME ❧

On the day when I faced disaster, they confronted me,
     but the LORD came to my defense.

Psalm 13:18

I trust you, O my God.
   Do not let me be put to shame.
   Do not let my enemies triumph over me.
No one who waits for you will ever be put to shame,
   but all who are unfaithful will be put to shame.

Psalm 25:2-3

I made my sins known to you; and I did not cover up my guilt.
I decided to confess them to you, O LORD.
   Then you forgave all my sins.

Psalm 32:5

All who look to him will be radiant.
   Their faces will never be covered with shame.

Psalm 34:5

The LORD is near to those whose hearts are humble.
He saves those whose spirits are crushed.

Psalm 34:18

Wash me thoroughly from my guilt,
   and cleanse me from my sin.
Purify me from sin with hyssop, and I will be clean.
Wash me, and I will be whiter than snow.

Psalm 51:2,7

As high as the heavens are above the earth—
    that is how vast his mercy is toward those who fear him.
As far as the east is from the west—
    that is how far he has removed our rebellious acts from himself.

Psalm 103:11-12

Then I will never feel ashamed
    when I study all your commandments.

Psalm 119:6

He was wounded for our rebellious acts.
He was crushed for our sins.
    He was punished so that we could have peace,
      and we received healing from his wounds.
    We have all strayed like sheep.
    Each one of us has turned to go his own way,
      and the LORD has laid all our sins on him.

Isaiah 53:5-6

I'm not ashamed of the Good News. It is God's power to save everyone
who believes, Jews first and Greeks as well.

Romans 1:16

Scripture says, "Whoever believes in him will not be ashamed."

Romans 10:11

Instead, we have refused to use secret and shameful ways. We don't use tricks, and we don't distort God's word. As God watches, we clearly reveal the truth to everyone.

2 Corinthians 4:2a

Do your best to present yourself to God as a tried-and-true worker who isn't ashamed to teach the word of truth correctly.

2 Timothy 2:15

❧ SICKNESS ❧

He said, "If you will listen carefully to the LORD your God and do what he considers right, if you pay attention to his commands and obey all his laws, I will never make you suffer any of the diseases I made the Egyptians suffer, because I am the LORD, who heals you."

Exodus 15:26

Be strong, all who wait with hope for the LORD,
    and let your heart be courageous.

Psalm 31:24

The LORD will support him on his sickbed.
    You will restore this person to health when he is ill.

Psalm 41:3

Praise the LORD, my soul,
    and never forget all the good he has done:

He is the one who forgives all your sins,
    the one who heals all your diseases.

Psalm 103:2-

He sent his message and healed them.
He rescued them from the grave.

Psalm 107:2

A joyful heart is good medicine,
    but depression drains one's strength.

Proverbs 17:2

Jesus went to all the towns and villages. He taught in the synagogues
and spread the Good News of the kingdom. He also cured every
disease and sickness.

Matthew 9:3

Praise the God and Father of our Lord Jesus Christ! He is the Father
who is compassionate and the God who gives comfort. He comforts us
whenever we suffer. That is why whenever other people suffer, we are
able to comfort them by using the same comfort we have received
from God.

2 Corinthians 1:3-

Prayers offered in faith will save those who are sick, and the Lord will
cure them.

James 5:15

∼ SORROW ∼

His anger lasts only a moment.
His favor lasts a lifetime.
  Weeping may last for the night,
    but there is a song of joy in the morning.

Psalm 30:5

You have changed my sobbing into dancing.
You have removed my sackcloth and clothed me with joy

Psalm 30:11

I will rejoice and be glad because of your mercy.
  You have seen my misery.
  You have known the troubles in my soul.

Psalm 31:7

The Lord is near to those whose hearts are humble.
He saves those whose spirits are crushed.

Psalm 34:18

Then young women will rejoice and dance
  along with young men and old men.
I will turn their mourning into joy.
I will comfort them.
I will give them joy in place of their sorrow.

Jeremiah 31:13

In fact, to be distressed in a godly way causes people to change the way they think and act and leads them to be saved. No one can regret that. But the distress that the world causes brings only death.

2 Corinthians 7:10

❧ STRENGTH ❧

Love the LORD your God with all your heart, with all your soul, and with all your strength.

Deuteronomy 6:5

The LORD's eyes scan the whole world to find those whose hearts are committed to him and to strengthen them.

2 Chronicles 16:9

I love you, O LORD, my strength.

Psalm 18:1

God arms me with strength
and makes my way perfect.

Psalm 18:32

God, the God of Israel, is awe-inspiring in his holy place.
He gives strength and power to his people.
Thanks be to God!

Psalm 68:35

My body and mind may waste away,
  but God remains the foundation of my life
    and my inheritance forever.

Psalm 73:26

The name of the LORD is a strong tower.
  A righteous person runs to it and is safe.

Proverbs 18:10

Yet, the strength of those who wait with hope in the LORD
  will be renewed.
    They will soar on wings like eagles.
      They will run and won't become weary.

Isaiah 40:31

They will walk and won't grow tired.
Don't be afraid, because I am with you.
Don't be intimidated; I am your God.
  I will strengthen you.
  I will help you.
  I will support you with my victorious right hand.

Isaiah 41:10

I can do everything through Christ who strengthens me.

Philippians 4:13

God our Father loved us and by his kindness gave us everlasting
encouragement and good hope. Together with our Lord Jesus Christ,
may he encourage and strengthen you to do and say everything that is
good.

2 Thessalonians 2:16-17

❧ STRESS ❧

I called on the LORD in my distress.
   I cried to my God for help.
      He heard my voice from his temple,
         and my cry for help reached his ears.

Psalm 18:6

Relieve my troubled heart,
   and bring me out of my distress.
Look at my misery and suffering,
   and forgive all my sins.

Psalm 25:17-18

Have pity on me, O LORD, because I am in distress.
   My eyes, my soul, and my body waste away from grief.

Psalm 31:9

My soul waits calmly for God alone.
   My salvation comes from him.

He alone is my rock and my savior—my stronghold.
   I cannot be severely shaken.

Psalm 62:1-2

Thanks be to the Lord,
   who daily carries our burdens for us.
      God is our salvation.

Psalm 68:19

When I worried about many things,
   your assuring words soothed my soul.

Psalm 94:19

When you go through the sea, I am with you.
When you go through rivers, they will not sweep you away.
When you walk through fire, you will not be burned,
   and the flames will not harm you.

Isaiah 43:2

Come to me, all who are tired from carrying heavy loads, and I will
give you rest.

Matthew 11:28

In every way we're troubled, but we aren't crushed by our troubles.
We're frustrated, but we don't give up. We're persecuted, but we're not
abandoned. We're captured, but we're not killed.

2 Corinthians 4:8-9

Never worry about anything. But in every situation let God know what you need in prayers and requests while giving thanks. Then God's peace, which goes beyond anything we can imagine, will guard your thoughts and emotions through Christ Jesus.

Philippians 4:6-7

 # STRIFE

See how good and pleasant it is
    when brothers and sisters live together in harmony!

Psalm 133:1

Whoever forgives an offense seeks love,
    but whoever keeps bringing up the issue
        separates the closest of friends.

Proverbs 17:9

Avoiding a quarrel is honorable.
    After all, any stubborn fool can start a fight.

Proverbs 20:3

As churning milk produces butter
    and punching a nose produces blood,
        so stirring up anger produces a fight.

Proverbs 30:33

Stop judging, and you will never be judged. Stop condemning, and you will never be condemned. Forgive, and you will be forgiven.

Luke 6:37

When you are jealous and quarrel among yourselves, aren't you influenced by your corrupt nature and living by human standards?

1 Corinthians 3:3b

Put up with each other, and forgive each other if anyone has a complaint. Forgive as the Lord forgave you.

Colossians 3:13

What causes fights and quarrels among you? Aren't they caused by the selfish desires that fight to control you?

James 4:1

❧ STRUGGLES ❧

The LORD is fighting for you! So be still!

Exodus 14:14

So I run—but not without a clear goal ahead of me. So I box—but not as if I were just shadow boxing.

1 Corinthians 9:26

This is not a wrestling match against a human opponent. We are wrestling with rulers, authorities, the powers who govern this world of darkness, and spiritual forces that control evil in the heavenly world.

Ephesians 6:12

I work hard and struggle to do this while his mighty power works in me.

Colossians 1:29

Fight the good fight for the Christian faith. Take hold of everlasting life to which you were called and about which you made a good testimony in front of many witnesses.

1 Timothy 6:12

You struggle against sin, but your struggles haven't killed you.

Hebrews 12:4

❧ STUBBORNNESS ❧

But my people did not listen to me.
   Israel wanted nothing to do with me.
      So I let them go their own stubborn ways
         and follow their own advice.

Psalm 81:11-12

Pride precedes a disaster,
   and an arrogant attitude precedes a fall.

Proverbs 16:18

They made their hearts as hard as flint so that they couldn't hear the LORD's teachings, the words that the LORD of Armies had sent by his Spirit through the earlier prophets. So the LORD of Armies became very angry.

Zechariah 7:12

Be careful, brothers and sisters, that none of you ever develop a wicked, unbelieving heart that turns away from the living God.

Hebrews 3:12

⇜ SUCCESS ⇝

Only be strong and very courageous, faithfully doing everything in the teachings that my servant Moses commanded you. Don't turn away from them. Then you will succeed wherever you go.

Joshua 1:7

Blessed is the person who does not
   follow the advice of wicked people,
     take the path of sinners,
       or join the company of mockers.
Rather, he delights in the teachings of the LORD

and reflects on his teachings day and night.
He is like a tree planted beside streams—
a tree that produces fruit in season
and whose leaves do not wither.
He succeeds in everything he does.

Psalm 1:1-3

He will give you your heart's desire
and carry out all your plans.

Psalm 20:4

Without advice plans go wrong,
but with many advisers they succeed.

Proverbs 15:22

Entrust your efforts to the LORD,
and your plans will succeed.

Proverbs 16:3

On the heels of humility (the fear of the LORD)
are riches and honor and life.

Proverbs 22:4

A trustworthy person has many blessings,
but anyone in a hurry to get rich will not escape punishment.

Proverbs 28:20

∽ SUFFERING ∽

You have heard the desire of oppressed people, O LORD.
You encourage them.
You pay close attention to them

Psalm 10:17

The LORD has not despised or been disgusted
  with the plight of the oppressed one.
    He has not hidden his face from that person.
      The LORD heard when that oppressed person
        cried out to him for help.

Psalm 22:24

Relieve my troubled heart,
  and bring me out of my distress.

Psalm 25:17

But that's not all. We also brag when we are suffering. We know that
suffering creates endurance, endurance creates character, and
character creates confidence.

Romans 5:3

I consider our present sufferings insignificant compared to the glory
that will soon be revealed to us.

Romans 8:18

God has given you the privilege not only to believe in Christ but also to suffer for him.

Philippians 1:29

If we endure, we will rule with him.
If we disown him, he will disown us.

2 Timothy 2:12

Turn all your anxiety over to God because he cares for you.

1 Peter 5:7

❧ TEMPTATION ❧

If you do well, won't you be accepted? But if you don't do well, sin is lying outside your door ready to attack. It wants to control you, but you must master it.

Genesis 4:7

There isn't any temptation that you have experienced which is unusual for humans. God, who faithfully keeps his promises, will not allow you to be tempted beyond your power to resist. But when you are tempted, he will also give you the ability to endure the temptation as your way of escape.

1 Corinthians 10:13

For this reason, take up all the armor that God supplies. Then you will be able to take a stand during these evil days. Once you have overcome all obstacles, you will be able to stand your ground.

Ephesians 6:13

After all, God's saving kindness has appeared for the benefit of all people. It trains us to avoid ungodly lives filled with worldly desires so that we can live self-controlled, moral, and godly lives in this present world.

Titus 2:11-12

Because Jesus experienced temptation when he suffered, he is able to help others when they are tempted.

Hebrews 2:18

You struggle against sin, but your struggles haven't killed you.

Hebrews 12:4

So place yourselves under God's authority. Resist the devil, and he will run away from you.

James 4:7

Keep your mind clear, and be alert. Your opponent the devil is prowling around like a roaring lion as he looks for someone to devour.

1 Peter 5:8

❧ THANKFULNESS ❧

I will give thanks to the LORD for his righteousness.
I will make music to praise the name of the LORD Most High.

Psalm 7:17

Enter his gates with a song of thanksgiving.
Come into his courtyards with a song of praise.
Give thanks to him; praise his name.

Psalm 100:4

Give thanks to the LORD because he is good,
    because his mercy endures forever.

Psalm 107:1

They knew God but did not praise and thank him for being God. Instead,
their thoughts were pointless, and their misguided minds were plunged
into darkness.

Romans 1:21

I thank my God for all the memories I have of you.

Philippians 1:3

Never worry about anything. But in every situation let God know what you
need in prayers and requests while giving thanks.

Philippians 4:6

Whatever happens, give thanks, because it is God's will in Christ Jesus that you do this.

1 Thessalonians 5:18

~ THOUGHTFULNESS ~

However, be careful, and watch yourselves closely so that you don't forget the things which you have seen with your own eyes. Don't let them fade from your memory as long as you live. Teach them to your children and grandchildren.

Deuteronomy 4:9

A gullible person believes anything,
     but a sensible person watches his step.

Proverbs 14:15

Now, this is what the LORD of Armies says: Carefully consider your ways!

Haggai 1:5

I can guarantee that on judgment day people will have to give an account of every careless word they say.

Matthew 12:36

So then, be very careful how you live. Don't live like foolish people but like wise people.

Ephesians 5:15

For this reason we must pay closer attention to what we have heard.
Then we won't drift away ⌊from the truth⌋.

Hebrews 2:1

 TRIALS

The victory for righteous people comes from the LORD.
He is their fortress in times of trouble.

Psalm 37:39

Because Christ suffered so much for us, we can receive so much
comfort from him.

2 Corinthians 1:5

Our suffering is light and temporary and is producing for us an eternal
glory that is greater than anything we can imagine.

2 Corinthians 4:17

Instead, our lives demonstrate that we are God's servants. We have
endured many things: suffering, distress, anxiety.

2 Corinthians 6:4

My brothers and sisters, be very happy when you are tested in
different ways.

James 1:2

Dear friends, don't be surprised by the fiery troubles that are coming in order to test you. Don't feel as though something strange is happening to you.

1 Peter 4:12

Since the Lord did all this, he knows how to rescue godly people when they are tested. He also knows how to hold immoral people for punishment on the day of judgment.

2 Peter 2:9

~ TROUBLES ~

Even though I walk through the dark valley of death,
    because you are with me, I fear no harm.
        Your rod and your staff give me courage.

Psalm 23:4

Relieve my troubled heart,
    and bring me out of my distress.

Psalm 25:17

Why are you discouraged, my soul?
Why are you so restless?
    Put your hope in God,
        because I will still praise him.
            He is my savior and my God.

Psalm 42:5

Turn your burdens over to the LORD,
  and he will take care of you.
    He will never let the righteous person stumble.

Psalm 55:22

This is my comfort in my misery:
  Your promise gave me a new life.

Psalm 119:50

Let your mercy comfort me
  as you promised.

Psalm 119:76

The LORD is good.
  ₍He is₎ a fortress in the day of trouble.
  He knows those who seek shelter in him.

Nahum 1:7

Come to me, all who are tired from carrying heavy loads, and I will
give you rest.

Matthew 11:28

Don't be troubled. Believe in God.

John 14:1

I'm leaving you peace. I'm giving you my peace. I don't give you the
kind of peace that the world gives. So don't be troubled or cowardly.

John 14:27

Praise the God and Father of our Lord Jesus Christ! He is the Father who is compassionate and the God who gives comfort. He comforts us whenever we suffer. That is why whenever other people suffer, we are able to comfort them by using the same comfort we have received from God.

2 Corinthians 1:3-4

❧ UNCERTAINTY ❧

No one knows when that day or hour will come. Even the angels in heaven and the Son don't know. Only the Father knows.

Matthew 24:36

Jesus said to them, "Have faith in God!"

Mark 11:22

However, he gave the right to become God's children to everyone who believed in him.

John 1:12

Jesus said to Thomas, "You believe because you've seen me. Blessed are those who haven't seen me but believe."

John 20:29

Faith assures us of things we expect and convinces us of the existence of things we cannot see.

Hebrews 11:1

Tell those who have the riches of this world not to be arrogant and not to place their confidence in anything as uncertain as riches. Instead, they should place their confidence in God who richly provides us with everything to enjoy.

1 Timothy 6:17

If any of you needs wisdom to know what you should do, you should ask God, and he will give it to you. God is generous to everyone and doesn't find fault with them. When you ask for something, don't have any doubts. A person who has doubts is like a wave that is blown by the wind and tossed by the sea. A person who has doubts shouldn't expect to receive anything from the Lord. A person who has doubts is thinking about two different things at the same time and can't make up his mind about anything.

James 1:5-8

❧ UNFAIRNESS ❧

"Because oppressed people are robbed and needy people groan,
   I will now arise," says the LORD.
"I will provide safety for those who long for it."

Psalm 12:5

No one who waits for you will ever be put to shame,
   but all who are unfaithful will be put to shame.

Psalm 25:3

This is what happens to everyone
   who is greedy for unjust gain.
      Greed takes away his life.

Proverbs 1:19

Dishonest scales are disgusting to the LORD,
   but accurate weights are pleasing to him.

Proverbs 11:1

Bless those who curse you. Pray for those who insult you.

Luke 6:28

∽ UNSURE ∽

But if you don't want to serve the LORD, then choose today whom you will serve. . . . My family and I will still serve the LORD.

Joshua 24:15

If I climb upward on the rays of the morning sun
   ⌊or⌋ land on the most distant shore of the sea where the sun sets,
      even there your hand would guide me
         and your right hand would hold on to me.

Psalm 139:9-10

Jesus said to them, "Have faith in God!"

Mark 11:22

That's why I tell you to have faith that you have already received whatever you pray for, and it will be yours.

Mark 11:24

[Abraham] didn't doubt God's promise out of a lack of faith. Instead, giving honor to God ⌊for the promise⌋, he became strong because of faith.

Romans 4:20

God saved you through faith as an act of kindness. You had nothing to do with it. Being saved is a gift from God.

Ephesians 2:8

The one who calls you is faithful.

1 Thessalonians 5:24a

Be careful, brothers and sisters, that none of you ever develop a wicked, unbelieving heart that turns away from the living God.

Hebrews 3:12

Faith assures us of things we expect and convinces us of the existence of things we cannot see.

Hebrews 11:1

When you ask for something, don't have any doubts. A person who has doubts is like a wave that is blown by the wind and tossed by the sea.

James 1:6

Although you have never seen Christ, you love him. You don't see him now, but you believe in him. You are extremely happy with joy and praise that can hardly be expressed in words as you obtain the salvation that is the goal of your faith.

1 Peter 1:8-9

∾ VICTORY ∾

Only be strong and very courageous, faithfully doing everything in the teachings that my servant Moses commanded you. Don't turn away from them. Then you will succeed wherever you go.

Joshua 1:7

Blessed is the person who does not
   follow the advice of wicked people,
      take the path of sinners,
         or join the company of mockers.
Rather, he delights in the teachings of the LORD
   and reflects on his teachings day and night.
He is like a tree planted beside streams—
   a tree that produces fruit in season
      and whose leaves do not wither.
He succeeds in everything he does.

Psalm 1:1-3

You have given me the shield of your salvation.
Your right hand supports me.
Your gentleness makes me great.

Psalm 18:35

With God we will display great strength.
   He will trample our enemies.

Psalm 60:12

A nation will fall when there is no direction,
   but with many advisers there is victory.

Proverbs 11:14

In the world you'll have trouble. But cheer up! I have overcome the
world.

John 16:33b

The one who loves us gives us an overwhelming victory in all these
difficulties.

Romans 8:37

When this body that decays is changed into a body that cannot decay,
and this mortal body is changed into a body that will live forever, then
the teaching of Scripture will come true:
   "Death is turned into victory!"

1 Corinthians 15:54

Thank God that he gives us the victory through our Lord Jesus Christ.

1 Corinthians 15:57

Everyone who has been born from God has won the victory over the world. Our faith is what wins the victory over the world. Who wins the victory over the world? Isn't it the person who believes that Jesus is the Son of God?

1 John 5:4-5

≈ VULNERABILITY ≈

But you, O LORD, are a shield that surrounds me.
    You are my glory.
    You hold my head high.

Psalm 3:3

You have seen ⌊it⌋; yes, you have taken note of trouble and grief
    and placed them under your control.
        The victim entrusts himself to you.
You alone have been the helper of orphans.

Psalm 10:14

"Because oppressed people are robbed and needy people groan,
    I will now arise," says the LORD.
    "I will provide safety for those who long for it."

Psalm 12:5

You have been my refuge,
a tower of strength against the enemy.

Psalm 61:3

They will not come near you,
even though a thousand may fall dead beside you
or ten thousand at your right side.

Psalm 91:7

When you go through the sea, I am with you.
When you go through rivers, they will not sweep you away.
When you walk through fire, you will not be burned,
and the flames will not harm you.

Isaiah 43:2

 WEAKNESS

The LORD is my light and my salvation.
Who is there to fear?
The LORD is my life's fortress.
Who is there to be afraid of?

Psalm 27:1

Blessed is the one who has concern for helpless people.
The LORD will rescue him in times of trouble.

Psalm 41:1

He will have pity on the poor and needy
and will save the lives of the needy.

Psalm 72:13

Defend weak people and orphans.
Protect the rights of the oppressed and the poor.

Psalm 82:3

When I called, you answered me.
You made me bold by strengthening my soul.

Psalm 138:3

Stay awake, and pray that you won't be tempted. You want to do what's right, but you're weak.

Matthew 26:41

At the same time the Spirit also helps us in our weakness, because we don't know how to pray for what we need. But the Spirit intercedes along with our groans that cannot be expressed in words.

Romans 8:26

But he told me: "My kindness is all you need. My power is strongest when you are weak." So I will brag even more about my weaknesses in order that Christ's power will live in me. Therefore, I accept weakness, mistreatment, hardship, persecution, and difficulties suffered for Christ. It's clear that when I'm weak, I'm strong.

2 Corinthians 12:9-10

We have a chief priest who is able to sympathize with our weaknesses.
He was tempted in every way that we are, but he didn't sin.

Hebrews 4:15

❧ WISDOM ❧

I will praise the LORD, who advises me.
  My conscience warns me at night.

Psalm 16:7

The teachings of the LORD are perfect.
  They renew the soul.
The testimony of the LORD is dependable.
  It makes gullible people wise.

Psalm 19:7

⌊The LORD says,⌋
  "I will instruct you.
  I will teach you the way that you should go.
  I will advise you as my eyes watch over you."

Psalm 32:8

Yet, you desire truth and sincerity.
  Deep down inside me you teach me wisdom.

Psalm 51:6

The fear of the LORD is the beginning of wisdom.
Good sense is shown by everyone
    who follows ⌊God's guiding principles⌋.
His praise continues forever.

Psalm 111:10

Blessed is the one who finds wisdom
    and the one who obtains understanding.

Proverbs 3:13

I pray that the glorious Father, the God of our Lord Jesus Christ,
would give you a spirit of wisdom and revelation as you come to know
Christ better.

Ephesians 1:17

God has hidden all the treasures of wisdom and knowledge in Christ.

Colossians 2:3

From infancy you have known the Holy Scriptures. They have the
power to give you wisdom so that you can be saved through faith in
Christ Jesus.

2 Timothy 3:15

If any of you needs wisdom to know what you should do, you should
ask God, and he will give it to you. God is generous to everyone and
doesn't find fault with them.

James 1:5

❧ WORRY ❧

Turn your burdens over to the LORD,
   and he will take care of you.
      He will never let the righteous person stumble.

Psalm 55:22

Thanks be to the Lord,
   who daily carries our burdens for us.
      God is our salvation.

Psalm 68:19

When I worried about many things,
   your assuring words soothed my soul.

Psalm 94:19

Can any of you add a single hour to your life by worrying?

Matthew 6:27

So don't ever worry about tomorrow. After all, tomorrow will worry
about itself. Each day has enough trouble of its own.

Matthew 6:34

Make sure that you don't become drunk, hung over, and worried about
life.

Luke 21:34a

Don't be troubled. Believe in God.

John 14:1a

My God will richly fill your every need in a glorious way through
Christ Jesus.

Philippians 4:19

Also, let Christ's peace control you. God has called you into this peace
by bringing you into one body. Be thankful.

Colossians 3:15

~ WORTHLESSNESS ~

You are a holy people, who belong to the LORD your God. He chose
you to be his own special possession out of all the nations on earth.

Deuteronomy 7:6

I will give thanks to you
    because I have been so amazingly and miraculously made.
        Your works are miraculous, and my soul is fully aware of this.

Psalm 139:14

Since you are precious to me, you are honored and I love you.
    I will exchange others for you.
        Nations will be the price I pay for your life.

Isaiah 43:4

Before I formed you in the womb,
   I knew you.
Before you were born,
   I set you apart for my holy purpose.
   I appointed you to be a prophet to the nations.

Jeremiah 1:5

The LORD appeared to me in a faraway place and said,
   "I love you with an everlasting love.
      So I will continue to show you my kindness."

Jeremiah 31:3

Aren't two sparrows sold for a penny? Not one of them will fall to the ground without your Father's permission. Every hair on your head has been counted. Don't be afraid! You are worth more than many sparrows.

Matthew 10:29, 31

You are all God's children by believing in Christ Jesus.

Galatians 3:26

Because you are God's children, God has sent the Spirit of his Son into us to call out, "Abba! Father!" So you are no longer slaves but God's children. Since you are God's children, God has also made you heirs.

Galatians 4:6-7

⚛ WRONGS ⚛

Those who brag cannot stand in your sight.
You hate all troublemakers.

Psalm 5:5

Do not remember the sins of my youth or my rebellious ways.
   Remember me, O LORD, in keeping with your mercy
      and your goodness.

Psalm 25:7

Blessed is the person whose disobedience is forgiven
   and whose sin is pardoned.
Blessed is the person whom the LORD no longer accuses of sin
   and who has no deceitful thoughts.

Psalm 32:1-2

I have sinned against you, especially you.
I have done what you consider evil.
   So you hand down justice when you speak,
      and you are blameless when you judge.

Psalm 51:4

As far as the east is from the west—
   that is how far he has removed our rebellious acts from himself.

Psalm 103:12

O LORD, who would be able to stand
    if you kept a record of sins?
But with you there is forgiveness
    so that you can be feared.

Psalm 130:3-4

Hate starts quarrels,
    but love covers every wrong.

Proverbs 10:12

[Love] isn't rude. It doesn't think about itself. It isn't irritable. It doesn't keep track of wrongs.

1 Corinthians 13:5

Make sure that no one ever pays back one wrong with another wrong. Instead, always try to do what is good for each other and everyone else.

1 Thessalonians 5:15

Every kind of wrongdoing is sin, yet there are sins that don't lead to death.

1 John 5:17

❧

If you have enjoyed *Promises from GOD'S WORD*, you may wish to consider using another Bible or devotional book that uses the *GOD'S WORD*™ text for the Bible. *GOD'S WORD*™ is the best-selling Bible translation that delivers God's message in crystal clear English.

Other *GOD'S WORD*™ products published by God's Word to the Nations Bible Society and World Publishing are available at your local Christian bookstore.

❧

Steps to Peace with God

 Step 1 God's Purpose:
Peace and Life

God loves you and wants you to experience peace and
life—abundant and eternal.

The Bible Says . . .

". . . we have peace with God through our Lord
Jesus Christ." Romans 5:1

"For God so loved the world that He gave His
only begotten Son, that whoever believes in Him
should not perish but have everlasting life."
John 3:16

". . . I have come that they may have life,
and that they may have it more abundantly."
John 10:10b

Since God planned
for us to have peace
and the abundant life
right now, why are
most people not hav-
ing this experience?

Step 2 | Our Problem: Separation

God created us in His own image to have an abundant life. He did not make us as robots to automatically love and obey Him, but gave us a will and a freedom of choice.

We chose to disobey God and go our own willful way. We still make this choice today. This results in separation from God.

The Bible Says . . .

"For all have sinned and fall short of the glory of God." Romans 3:23

"For the wages of sin is death, but the gift of God is eternal life in Christ Jesus our Lord." Romans 6:23

Our choice results in separation from God.

Our Attempts

Through the ages, individuals have tried in many ways to bridge this gap . . . without success . . .

The Bible Says . . .

"There is a way that seems right to man, but in the end it leads to death." Proverbs 14:12

"But your iniquities have separated you from God; and your sins have hidden His face from you, so that He will not hear." Isaiah 59:2

There is only one remedy for this problem of separation.

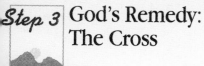

Step 3 God's Remedy: The Cross

Jesus Christ is the only answer to this problem. He died on the Cross and rose from the grave, paying the penalty for our sin and bridging the gap between God and people.

The Bible Says . . .

". . . God is on one side and all the people on the other side, and Christ Jesus, Himself man, is between them to bring them together . . ." 1 Timothy 2:5

"For Christ also has suffered once for sins, the just for the unjust, that He might bring us to God . . ." 1 Peter 3:18a

"But God demonstrates His own love for us in this: While we were still sinners, Christ died for us." Romans 5:8

God has provided the only way . . . we must make the choice . . .

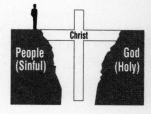

Step 4
Our Response: Receive Christ

We must trust Jesus Christ and receive Him by personal invitation.

The Bible Says . . .

"Behold, I stand at the door and knock. If anyone hears My voice and opens the door, I will come in to him and dine with him, and he with Me." Revelation 3:20

"But as many as received Him, to them He gave the right to become children of God, even to those who believe in His name." John 1:12

". . . if you confess with your mouth the Lord Jesus and believe in your heart that God has raised Him from the dead, you will be saved." Romans 10:9

Are you here . . . or here?

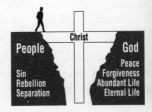

Is there any good reason why you cannot receive Jesus Christ right now?

How to receive Christ:

1. Admit your need (I am a sinner).
2. Be willing to turn from your sins (repent).
3. Believe that Jesus Christ died for you on the Cross and rose from the grave.
4. Through prayer, invite Jesus Christ to come in and control your life through the Holy Spirit. (Receive Him as Lord and Savior.)

What to Pray:

Dear Lord Jesus,

I know that I am a sinner and need Your forgiveness. I believe that You died for my sins. I want to turn from my sins. I now invite You to come into my heart and life. I want to trust and follow You as Lord and Savior.

In Jesus' name. Amen.

_____   _____
Date   Signature

God's Assurance: His Word

If you prayed this prayer,

The Bible Says...

"For 'whoever calls upon the name of the Lord will be saved.'" Romans 10:13

Did you sincerely ask Jesus Christ to come into your life? Where is He right now? What has He given you?

"For it is by grace you have been saved, through faith—and this is not from yourselves, it is the gift of God—not by works, so that no one can boast." Ephesians 2:8,9